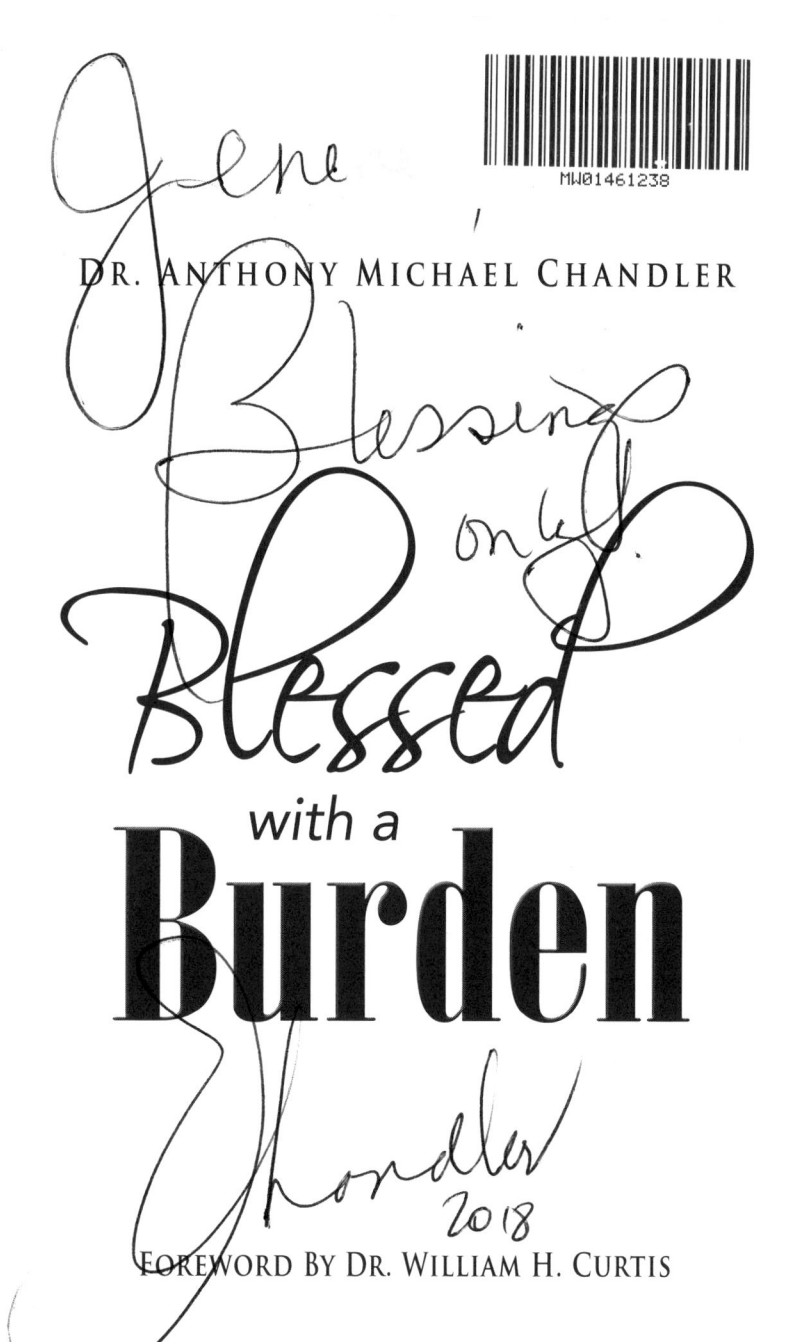

DR. ANTHONY MICHAEL CHANDLER

Blessed
with a
Burden

FOREWORD BY DR. WILLIAM H. CURTIS

Copyright © 2012 by Anthony Michael Chandler, Sr., D.Min.

All rights reserved. No part of this book may be used, reproduced, stored in a retrieval system, or transmitted in any form whatsoever — including electronic, photocopy, recording — without prior written permission from the author, except in the case of brief quotations embodied in critical articles or reviews.

All scripture quotations, unless otherwise indicated, are taken from *The Message*. Copyright © 1993, 1994, 1995, 1996, 2000, 2001, 2002. Used by permission of NavPress Publishing Group.

Additional Scripture quotations are taken from the *Holy Bible, King James Version*. KJV. Public Domain; and the *Holy Bible, New International Version*®. NIV®. Copyright © 1973, 1978, 1984 by International Bible Society. Used by permission of Zondervan. All rights reserved.

SECOND EDITION

ISBN: 978-1-936989-47-8

Library of Congress Control Number: 2012935725

Published by

Certa
PUBLISHING

P.O. Box 2839, Apopka, FL 32704

Printed in the United States of America

Disclaimer: The views and opinions expressed in this book are solely those of the authors and other contributors. These views and opinions do not necessarily represent those of Certa Publishing.

"I'm only in competition with myself!"

My most treasured lesson from Scotty J.

In memory of my grandfather, Mr. Earl King Spicer, who lived life well, loved his family unconditionally and spoke the truth without fear and the late Deaconess Bernice Tyson, who was the first person to carry me to church.

This book is dedicated to my pastor and spiritual father, Bishop Aggie L. Brown, Sr. who for over 30 years was able to bear the burden of ministry with integrity, compassion and humility. Thank you for your wisdom, guidance and the plethora of opportunities for me to hone and practice using my gifts.

Acknowledgements

God is Absolutely Awesome!

Amongst my mentors, spiritual parents, colleagues and friends, there are a few astute, God-fearing men who continue to bear the burden of ministry relentlessly and who allowed me to practice my gifts in some form as part of their ministries:

Bishop Oscar E. Brown remains iconic as both a pastor and preacher and was also the first pastor to extend ministerial opportunity, exposure, wisdom, and an uncompromising example of what EXCELLENCE in ministry should be. I'll never forget your words, "Before you stand, make sure that you know it. If you know it, they'll get it!" **Dr. James E. King** remains a trusted confidant, a true non-traditional, forward-thinker, who lives life without apology and the first pastor to think it not robbery to place me on the payroll and always claim me as his son. Thank you for introducing me to Proverbs 18:16. **Dr. Elmore E. Warren,** unselfishly and sagaciously, provided me a pastoral foundation, training and platform that enabled my voice to be heard in Baltimore and my territory enlarged in Richmond. **Bishop Walter Scott Thomas** has remained for me the model pastor of the 21st century. Bishop, I aspire to be the pastor you are. You value people and never meet a stranger. Thanks for allowing me to be a part of the family. I hope you appreciate the nuggets unearthed from *Good Meat Makes Its Own Gravy*. **Dr. A. Lincoln James**

has honored me by serving as my Richmond pastor. Your thunderous voice and preaching prowess are so remarkable. As a freshman in college, I couldn't wait to come to Trinity. **Dr. Lance Watson**, thank you for modeling integrity and remaining relevant. I'm on your heels. **Dr. Aggie L. Brown, Jr.**, **Dr. Russell L. Johnson** and **Dr. Leonard Smith** your investment in my life will never be forgotten. Thank you!

The following pastors have willingly shared the burdens and blessings of ministry with me: **Bishop Michael E. Dantley, Ed.D.**, you have saved my life! God strategically placed you in my life and you've been a catalyst of spiritual insight in understanding that "spiritual stuff"! Thank you for being a father. **Dr. William Curtis and Rev. Jimmy Baldwin,** you make the art of preaching seem so easy. Thank you for maintaining and setting a new standard for what traditional 'black' preaching should be. **Dr. Hoffman Brown**, your insightful and acute qualities are exceptional. My spiritual parents, **Drs. Stanley and Ann Fuller**, thank you for impressing upon me the value of rest and relaxation. **Dr. Jamal Bryant**, you've made myriad deposits in my life and ministry. You once shared with me, "If you don't want God to do it, don't ask me to pray." He certainly answers your prayers. My wonderful in-loves, **Pastor Lee and Evangelist Judith Pearson, Mr. Keith Miller, Rev. Tyrone Thomas, Dr. Derik Jones, Dr. Damon Peterson, Rev. Darryl Gould, Deacon Eric Taylor, Minister James Johnson, Rev. Vernon Shelton, Rev. Phillip Deal** and **Mr. Jonathan Coleman (and my other early morning gym (prison) partners)**, your continued friendship and involvement in my life has made bearing this burden less cumbersome.

Without you, this wouldn't have happened! My wife, Taleshia, has been my encourager, helper, companion and best friend. She is unequivocally the smartest woman I know. Her intellect, beauty, and individualism have remained unwavering and impressive. Thank you for sharing this wonderful journey with me. I can't imagine life without you. My chickadees, A.K.A., the 'A-Team,' Anthony, Alysha and Andrew have enabled me to be the man I am. I love you all with every ounce of my being. Thank you for giving me a reason to want to live a long life.

My mother, the Queen, is without reservation the strongest and most courageous woman on earth. Thank you for never allowing me to settle for mediocrity. You are a tough cookie! You did that single mothering *thang* so well! Your house is on the way! Daddy-O, thanks for experiencing that call moment with me. The older I get, the more of a Daddy's boy I am. Daddy, thank you for always being there, even when you weren't supposed to be there. You never denied me. I'm thankful that we are making up each year for lost time! I am appreciative that my brothers and my only sister have always allowed me to simply be "Tony". Thank you Ricky for teaching me that *"it's not the size of the dog in the fight, but the fight that's in the dog!"*

My editors and readers: **Dee Wallain, Deaconess Etta V. Butler** (I will never forget your sacrifice and listening ear…you are amazing), **Mother Jean Braxton** (you know!), **Dr. Michael Dantley** (Bishop Father), **Dr. William Curtis** (my big brother and mentor) and my unwavering best friend and brother from another mother, **Dr. Vernon Walton**. Your sacrifice and revisions will always be treasured. Thank you, **Rev. June Rice, Rev. Steve Parker** and **Rev. James Briggs** for your thoughts on the theme.

The New Bethlehem Baptist Church was the church that taught me how to preach and pastor God's people. Walking away was the most difficult moment of this journey. Thank you for continuing to grow and become everything God has destined you to be.

The greatest and most fulfilling ministry opportunity that God has afforded me has been to pastor and serve as the 10th pastor of the Cedar Street Baptist Church of God in Richmond, Virginia. I am able to lead God's people with the greatest and most sincere group of church leaders. Thank you for trusting my leadership and gifts. So many of you (leaders and members) consistently hounded me and encouraged me to complete this task. Thanks for the PUSH! I wouldn't trade anything for this journey. I absolutely love *Living, Learning and Loving* with you. You are my blessing!

Dr. Anthony Michael Chandler, Sr.

Contents

Foreword by Dr. William H. Curtis 3

Introduction: The Burden Bearers 5

Chapter 1: The Burden Of Bearing Secrets 13

Chapter 2: The Burden Of A Transfer 25

Chapter 3: The Burden Of Arrival
There's A New Kid On The Block 47

Chapter 4: The Burden To Follow:
Honoring Your Predecessor 67

Chapter 5: The Burden To Empower Others 83

Chapter 6: The Burden To Find The Right Help 97

Chapter 7: The Burden Of Overcoming
The Chattering Crowd 117

Chapter 8: The Burden To Balance:
A Thorn, A Theory, A Testimony 133

Foreword

I discerned very early that Dr. Anthony Chandler possessed an unusual gift for transitioning traditional churches. The unique care of the people, while at the same time providing the necessary push to accept the "new wine skins" ministry needed was more than skill for him. It was clear then and confirmed with this much needed work that Dr. Chandler has been given a gift.

Story after story is told of the struggles that exist between pastors and their congregations. While there are many reasons for this, one of the seldom accepted realities is that transitioning takes skill and grace. It may be that the church invites the presence of the pastor's vision and the novelty of his or her ideas, as long as those ideas don't mess with the sacred pillars or practices and methods that have been held dear by that congregation long before the pastor arrived. Dr. Chandler has proven in two significant churches that the care of the soul and the shifting of an institution don't have to be mutually exclusive.

The principles he offers in this much needed work will provide you a time- proven, context-driven model for painlessly leading your congregation through transition. In both of his pastorates, I was refreshingly surprised observing the continual health of the congregations while at the same time noticing the changes that took place; many of which were the very reasons other pastors found themselves in the middle of church fights. It was then that I started really paying attention to what Dr. Chandler was doing, his methods of communicating and the shaping of His agenda. While working with pastors across the country, many of whom are walking into a context that needs transition in order to survive, I have directed them to observe very carefully the leadership of Dr. Chandler. Read his work, be blessed by his devotion to God, care for the people of God and his boldness to demand that a church stay relevant and faithful. Trust me; you will agree he is the resource we need for taking our churches forward.

                                      Blessings,
                                      Dr. William H. Curtis
                                      Senior Pastor
                                      "The Mount"

INTRODUCTION:

The Burden Bearers

"A man's gift maketh room for him and bringeth him before great men."

Proverbs 18:16

Introduction: The Burden Bearers

Life is completed by the challenges of the unknown and the burden of the seen. Blessings and burdens seem to be the order of the day and the responsibility of balancing them is ours. Faith, trust in God and prayer remain useful tools in maintaining a level head. However, while prayer is the key, it has also become the conduit of added pressures, disappointments and failure, for asking suggests that you expect to receive. The old adage "watch what you pray for" is certainly an understatement. For the reality is this--you just might get it. Am I suggesting that we withhold prayer? Of course not! To suggest that we withhold prayer is just as absurd as suggesting that all prayers will be answered. Not so! God hears all of our prayers, but His response is not always necessarily in the affirmative or negative.

God responds to our prayers. Oftentimes the response is in the affirmative. Yes, He responds to our prayers. His response may not be the answer we were expecting, but He is God and by virtue of His position as Creator, without argument, affords Him the privilege of being God. Have you ever wondered what God is thinking, especially when hearing our requests? I'm sure He laughs and must occasionally pause to say, if they only knew what they were asking.

Anyone who has ever been privileged to be in the

company of a sanctified person has heard them say, "God is in the blessing business."

However, has God's responding and answering our prayers presented or placed us in a position where what we believed to be a blessing, has become for us another burden? Wisdom tells us that every opportunity is not necessarily a blessing. Maybe we really should watch what we pray for because the fact is this, we just might have our prayers answered and often times to our detriment.

It is my belief that every blessing has the proclivity of also being a burden. Think about it. If you're married, you love your spouse, and you've made a public commitment to love *for better or for worse*. I once performed a wedding ceremony and the couple asked that I remove all of the negatives (sickness, worse, poorer); I responded absolutely not! I don't know of any couple who has escaped the adverse moments of marriage. Subsequently, I know of more couples who've been able to overcome the adverse moments of matrimonial bliss than those who've not been as successful.

Is life really just a journey of tests? Could a definition of life really be – strength on trial? The greatest among us have even declared what doesn't kill you only makes you stronger. Are you serious? There's an old adage that says, "Life was made for thinking. I think, so am I."

Why is ministry both a blessing and a burden?

What a blessing it is to be called into the ministry by God and to be called regardless of emotional frailties, physical flaws and occasional faults. It helps to validate your personhood, showing that God can use those who may seem ordinary and unusable in the eyes of humankind. It heightens your sense of purpose knowing that you are part of someone's salvation, emancipation, sanctification and transformation. It hurls you into that area of peace that surpasses all understanding; because, you are doing what God told you to do with the realization that ministry is also a burden. It is the burden of carrying a type of responsibility that can get too tough to fulfill and too tiresome to endure. It is also burdensome because ministry can be a road of travel that is often tremendously lonely and comes with a level of rejection that leads to many tearful times.

Some of the Challenges of Ministry

1. Maintaining balance between marriage/family and ministry

2. Discovering and being true to your own authentic gifts

3. Finding (good) mentors who are willing to invest in a relationship with you

4. Working with people who are content with the status quo (i.e. people who don't want to be and do greater things for God)

Some of the Opportunities of Ministry

1. The opportunity to devote your life to that which is of the utmost importance (serving God versus working in an unfulfilling job)

2. The opportunity to be used by God to transform lives and the world in unimaginable ways

3. The opportunity to develop lasting relationships with like-minded people

4. The opportunity to serve God in different ways (for

example, ministering in the church, the academy, para-church organizations, chaplaincy, etc.)

Some of the Misnomers of Ministry

1. Everyone to whom and with whom you minister shares your beliefs and values
2. People go into ministry because they can't do anything else
3. Everyone in ministry is rich and/or money-hungry
4. Ministers are naturally and necessarily "super-spiritual"
5. Ministry does not necessitate preparation, only an anointing

Some of the Opposing Forces of Ministry

1. Traditionalism (which is not the same as tradition)
2. Impure motives; immorality
3. Biblical illiteracy
4. Lack of spiritual discipline
5. Competition in the pulpit

Ministry is like a train transporting its constituents or contents where they or it needs to go while trying to stay on track. The challenge is maintaining smooth momentum. There is the challenge of attempting to please passengers (parishioners) who have the misconception that one's call means they are sinless, "super-nice heroes" who shouldn't ever be troubled or tired by their attitudes and ingratitude. The role of being the leader, minister or CEO is often such a "thankless" reality and there is the increasing challenge of hauling freight cars (loads) of others financial strains and mental stresses when there are occasions that you are just as broke and bewildered as they are. It is a challenge knowing you are connected to military cars (opposing forces) full of mean-hearted, nay-saying artillery ready to explode over not getting their way when one is in the middle of ministering and expected to do it with a spirit of excellence. I say these challenges are opportunities to demonstrate a faith that will motivate God's favor, dignity that will fuel your destiny and integrity that will be a testimony for another individual.

An additional challenge of ministry is trying to balance enough time for family, friends and fun. Those in ministry want to and should have the privilege of "going out to play" with those who they are in relationship with just like those who are not in ministry.

Personally, ministry is a blessing in the sense that God has decided to use us as agents of His transforming grace. For many, it is nothing short of a blessing to know that despite imperfections, ineptitudes and inclinations, God still chooses to use us in His service. The privilege to serve in ministry is a blessing in that it serves as yet another extension of God's grace.

Globally, ministry is a blessing in the sense that God has given us the opportunity to live as dispensers of His transforming grace. In my view, God has blessed us to bless others by sharing the Good News of His grace – grace that He first allows us to experience. For many, ministry is a burden because we are entrusted with the responsibility of carrying the life-giving and glorious grace of God to dying people. To unwrap this, let me first point out that Biblically, "glory" is a term that connotes weight (often indicating value or importance). Second, let me also explain that I understand the glory of God as being personally manifested in Christ. Therefore, ministry can be nothing less than a burden.

Ministry is the act of carrying a weight that is humanly unbearable. Thank God for Jesus who sits on the right hand of the Father, continually making intercession for us. For many, the greatest burden experienced in ministry is often bearing the weight of others. Subsequently, the love that people have for the minister is such a strong love that it causes them to have loftier expectations for the preacher than perhaps they should. They consequently expect the preacher to be more like God than Jesus. This phenomenon has become pandemic even for the preacher who continues to tirelessly be all things to all people.

Theologians have long discovered that Jesus was fully human, yet, He was also fully divine. God has been and will always be a fully divine spirit. People's thoughts and concerns towards the minister's attitude or regarding the minister's behavior serves as a clear indicator of how easily they either forget or fail to realize the human element that this person (the minister) fosters in their natural being. It is almost as though they expect the minister to be better than Jesus.

Of our own strength, no human is qualified or capable of carrying the weight of God's grace in Christ to the world. But, when God calls us, He also strengthens us. Paul may have said it best when he said, "In our weakness is His strength made perfect."

So, to those of us whom God has called, we carry the weight not of our own sufficiency, but understanding that our sufficiency is of God. The call to ministry is a blessing and a burden, but they are both necessary to further the Gospel, bearing fruit (the saving of souls) and the fullness of joy. Maybe instead of meandering around the burdens that accompany the call, we should view the call and mantle of our assignment through the eyes of God and not our own. At the end of the day, the reward will be bestowed upon the good and faithful one. I submit to you that ministry is workable and worth it.

Thank God that you have been blessed with such a burden!

Chapter One

The Burden Of Bearing Secrets

"Voice your outrage. Say it over and over, write it down and burn it in a bonfire, vent to your best friend, or scream it to your counselor. LIFE ISN'T FAIR. Get it out of your system as much and as regularly as you need to, but do not allow this truth to halt you in your progress forward."

Bishop T. D. Jakes
Senior Pastor, The Potter's House
Dallas, Texas

Chapter One ~ The Burden Of Bearing Secrets

I wonder how my parents felt on the day that I was born. My mother, a 20-year-old cosmetology student, had just buried her husband less than a year prior to my birth. My father, eight years her senior, the man who became her comforter after the funeral, was not present at the delivery, primarily because he had a wife and children who knew nothing about "the other woman." Listening to their stories today, my mother says that she never loved my father; he was just the "working man" who captivated her attention by the weight of his wallet and his manly countenance. My father was infatuated with my mother's beauty and her lady-like charm; but the striking reality remained, he was a married man who had just become the father of another woman's child. Go figure! I was **the child of the "other" woman**. That will most likely be the title of my next book. It really sounds like a good lifetime movie.

As I was saying, neither of my parents could deal with this dilemma. I was later informed by both of them, that my father made several attempts to father me. He even purchased my crib, so my mother said. Just weeks after I was born, my parents had a major confrontation. I was told the conversation went like this: my father told my mother that she would not be able to raise me without him. My mother concluded by saying, "Watch me and see!" From that day on, the secret had begun.

As a result of their inability to handle and confront the situation, I grew up in a family that was dealing with a secret. Approximately eighteen months past my birthday, my mother gave birth to my brother. My mother loved my brother's father dearly. Therefore, he did not just become my brother's biological father, but for me, an eighteen- month old, he was all I knew as a father. The day my brother was born was the day the secret actually began. I was now sharing his father as my own.

As strange as it seems, I remember the feelings of uncertainty as it related to the father that my brother and I shared. I always speculated that he wasn't my biological father. I was convinced that my mother's deceased husband was my "real" dad. So, for the sake of sparing my feelings, I just concluded that my family kept me uninformed to assist me in handling a potentially harrowing, emotional experience. I should also mention that my mother kept close ties with her in-laws. My brother and I were nurtured as part of their family. My mother even gave me her married name, which unsurprisingly strengthened the bond with this family. This was another factor that convinced me that my "real" father was deceased. The reality was this. I had his last name.

I grew up in a family where deception was not tolerated, or so I thought.

I grew up always wishing that I had another father, one other than the person who I was now living with and calling "daddy." I was the oldest son. I often imagined what it would be like to have older brothers and sisters. I desperately wanted and wished for something more than what I had.

~ 15 ~

As previously stated, my brother and I were extremely close to my mother's in-laws. Her mother-in-law, whom we affectionately called "Grandma," was a person who I loved dearly. I spent countless moments with her. She was our daycare provider. I can vividly remember the conversations we would have. We promised that we would always be true to each other. I grew up in a family where deception was not tolerated, or so I thought. If we were caught in a tale, the consequences were severe. I mean, really severe. Not abusive, just severe. This is so paradoxical, but you get the point.

One day in particular, I decided to confront her, my grandmother, with many of the hidden questions that I had dealt with internally regarding this person, my "real" father. I had the confidence then that I wish I had while writing this book. With no hesitation I asked her one afternoon, "Is he (my mother's deceased husband) my real father?" After a very brief pause, she agitatedly replied, "No!" I then took a leap of faith and asked her, "Well, is he (my brother's father) my 'real' father?"

For the first time in my life, I saw one of the strongest persons on earth gazing speechlessly. It was at that moment, she finally concluded that she could no longer keep this secret from me. It was evident by her response that she wasn't concerned about what my mother would think if she should find out that I now knew the truth. My grandmother realized that enough was enough. She responded to my question, "No, he isn't your father either!" I was again speechless. I was only eleven years old, and I was confused and angry, but as strange as it sounds, I wanted to know my real father's identity.

That night I confronted my mother with the same question I had posed earlier to my grandmother. I asked, "Is the man I call "Daddy" really my father?" After getting over her initial shock and moments of bewilderment, my mother's response to that question was "No, he isn't." Again, deception was never tolerated in my family. Although this was probably the day and conversation that my mother always wanted to avoid, I can now say that her queenly standards and integrity afforded me one of my earliest lessons of honesty. That night, my mother informed me I was asking the question seven months too early. She said that both she and my brother's father, from whom she was now separated due to his struggle with substance abuse, were going to break the family secrets as a present to me on my twelfth birthday. I guess I was six months too soon in breaking into a family secret.

I never imagined that before the night would end that multiple family secrets would be exposed. After my mother told me the truth about my biological father, she went on to reveal even more secrets. I learned that my grandfather, the man I thought to be her father and the gentleman who I respected more than any man on earth at that time, was actually her stepfather. There were more secrets shared which can't be penned in this book for fear of being alienated from my family. Needless to say, after that conversation with my mother, I was now a person in shock.

As we ended our conversation of revealing family secrets, my mother shared pictures with me of my biological father prior to my birth. The pictures were in a photo album that I had viewed on numerous occasions, but I had no idea who he was. I actually never paid any attention to the pictures of him. At this point, I was excited about meeting this man. He was tall, strong, and handsome, and I was told that he was great with handling his *change*. Strangely, yet obviously, everyone in my family knew who my father was, except for me and my younger family members. My entire family and even the neighbors next door were in on the secret. However, once the truth was revealed, I began informing my family that the secret was out. I wanted each of them to tell me everything they knew about him.

I learned that my biological father was the man who would occasionally drive by, say hello and place a five or twenty dollar bill in my hand. I was told that he once attended an elementary school math contest in which I participated. My father even told me, unbeknownst to my mother of course, that the two of us once had a conversation as I was standing on the corner near my house, a corner which he frequently passed. The more I talked with my family, the more I learned. It was now a mandate that I should meet this man. They all agreed with the same premise--my father was bald, suave and paid! I was told that he once was a boxer and upon my knowledge of him, he worked as a longshoreman. Notably, another fascinating truth pertaining to my father was that I was his youngest child. Yes, this meant that I actually had older brothers and sisters.

A few days later, my mother began the process of scheduling a time for the three of us to meet. Of course she wasn't going to allow this meeting to take place in her absence. My mother has always been extremely independent, outspoken and very protective of her two sons. As a single mother, discipline, respect and adherence to her many rules were never optional for me and my younger brother. A medal of honor should be awarded her for being the model mother and head of household, even as a single mother.

"Her sons rise up and call her blessed."

Proverbs 31:28

~ 18 ~

One day, actually two days before the Christmas of 1984, my grandfather, well, my step-grandfather and I were riding in his car a few blocks away from our home on Appleton Street in West Baltimore. From a distance, I saw a tall, handsome, bald man wearing a black leather jacket standing outside of a double-parked, black car. I took a guess and said, "Granddaddy, is that him?" After my grandfather had taken a glance at the man, he slammed on brakes, made a U-turn and drove to where the man stood. He instructed me to get out of the car, and then he looked at the man and said, "Sonny, (which was the man's nickname) this is your son. Tony, this is your father." I can't even describe how surreal that moment was for me. When I was introduced to him by my grandfather, my father's response to me was, "I've always known you, even though you didn't know who I was." He then gave me his phone number, he received mine and that was the beginning of a growing relationship.

From that day on, my father and I began our new relationship with each other. Although, I am convinced that all things work for good, there have been days when I have felt extremely angry towards both my mother and my biological father. There was anger towards my mother because she kept my father away from me. Simultaneously, there was similar anger towards my father for his parental absence.

> "There is no more vital calling or vocation for men than fathering."
>
> — John R. Throop

I can't help but think what might have happened if he had been in my life since birth. He was an athlete, yet I am now 38 years old and I still cannot play basketball. As a child, I was always considered the "mama's boy" while my brother and his father shared many intimate moments together as father and son. To my recollection, my brother's father fathered me to the best of his ability, yet there was a void that I now understand clearly. I have always been so desperate to have friendships with older people just so I'd be considered the "younger brother" in the crowd. Would my father and I be closer than we are now, had I spent my entire life with him? I longed for the safety and security a boy gets from having a father to protect him and keep him safe. When I was seven, I was molested by an older relative. I longed for a closer relationship with my older siblings. I became so desperate for the acceptance of others that I permitted myself to engage in unethical hazing practices just so I would be accepted by a fraternity. If I had had my dad earlier, would I have had a healthy sense of self? Would I have been able to say "no" to the things that made me feel uncomfortable? Would I have been able to seek his help when I felt threatened and tempted into gray areas? Perhaps I wouldn't have been so desperate for the attention and acceptance of others when what they wanted me to indulge in was wrong. Perhaps with my father's presence, love and support, it would have strengthened and sustained me in my years of faith and values formation. I am sure I spent years trying to bury the grief from this missing part of my early years.

In the past few years, however, there has been much progress made as my father and I have sought to strengthen our relationship. After high school, my mother even consented and supported me in changing my last name to my father's surname. For the most part, we manage a healthy relationship, which seems to only become quarrelsome when he speaks of the years I was apart from him. One very vivid memory that is prevalent in my mind is my wedding day in

November of 1996. On that special day, the day I married my high school sweetheart, my father kissed me and told me how proud he was to be my father.

As I developed this spiritual autobiography, for the first time I received this congruent revelation. Ironically, I was raised in a home with Christian values and traditions (gospel music on Sunday, no bike riding, no ironing, no work, etc.), even though my family was not, at that time, active in a local church. However, there was a neighbor who allowed the neighborhood children; me included, to attend church with her every Sunday. Interestingly, I was introduced to my father in December 1984, but more significantly, I established my personal relationship with Christ, a month prior in November 1984. I have actually known my biological father just as long as I've known my pastor and spiritual father.

Over the next five years, my relationship grew with both my spiritual father (pastor) and biological father. While developing a relationship with my biological father, my relationship with God was also deepened. I began serving in several capacities (i.e., as an usher, Sunday School leader, and as the youngest ordained junior deacon in Baltimore). Subsequently, my mother, who re-dedicated her life to God, became a member of the same church months later. Although the years lost between my father and I can never be reclaimed, a healing and a remnant of forgiveness had begun as I developed my relationship with God.

In December 1989 at the age of 16, I was convinced that God was calling me to a greater work. That very same month after a year of convincing experiences, I acknowledged my call to the gospel ministry. There was no traumatic moment or act of God that compelled me to acknowledge my call. There was just an internal flame and a yielding to the Spirit of God that convicted me to "Go ye therefore…" I preached my initial sermon one and a half years later. It was the same month I graduated from high school (Baltimore Polytechnic Institute) and two months prior to entering Virginia Union University.

In conclusion, I still can't offer an explanation as to why my life began the way it did. What was God preparing me for? Was this a burden or a blessing? What would be my raison d'être (my reason for being)? However as time passed, God's plan has been revealed. Not only was my father able to restore our relationship, he has also restored relations with my older brothers and sister. Today my father stands as one of the strongest supporters of my ministry. When I acknowledged my call, he said to me, "If you are going to be a preacher, tell the truth and be the best preacher that you can be so that one day, you can possibly save me."

That experience has certainly made me a better person and a stronger man. I am passionate concerning my role as father to my children. I have committed to not just being a sperm donor, but an active participant in their nurturance and spiritual development. I was there to save my oldest son when he was three-years old, when he jumped into a pool of deep water while on vacation. I was present for and survived the birth of my daughter as my wife delivered her on the front seat of our truck. Our youngest son, who was wrongfully pre-diagnosed as being born with Down's syndrome, has afforded my wife and I memorable moments in the emergency room. I'm blessed with a beautiful wife and wonderful, healthy children who we affectionately call our "A Team."

One of the greatest moments of my life was the first Sunday of April 2000. I began my first pastorate as the second pastor of the New Bethlehem Church in Baltimore.

In this role, I succeeded a founding pastor who pastored the congregation for more than 48 years. While serving as the youth pastor of another church in Baltimore, which enabled me to both appreciate and accept a more traditional style of worship and ministry, members of New Bethlehem heard my voice on the weekly Sunday morning broadcast. I was divinely employed and was honored to serve along with a senior pastor who afforded me some of his "radio time" which inevitably advanced my career opportunities and allowed my voice to be heard.

After a brief interview process, I was called to serve as the pastor of New Bethlehem Baptist Church at the age of 26. On my first Sunday after I delivered my initial pastoral message, the first person to accept Christ as personal savior and to obtain membership under my pastoral leadership was my father.

To this end, with so much transparency, I fully expose a few of my family secrets!

Chapter Two

The Burden Of A Transfer

"When I became a senior pastor, I began to realize just how clueless I really was. Seminary provided me with great knowledge, but still didn't prepare me. There is only one way to learn to navigate the challenges of church leadership – by doing it."

Pastor Ed Young
Senior Pastor of the Fellowship Church
Dallas/Fort Worth, Texas

Chapter Two ~ The Burden Of A Transfer

One of the most honored, yet thankless occupations, is to be called to serve as the spokesperson for God. Indeed, God speaks in ways unbeknownst to the articulatory altitudes of man which causes faith leaders to wonder is our being really necessary. Nevertheless, God has chosen many to serve as mouthpieces and agents of change for Kingdom expansion.

As with most employment query and unless you've been identified as the heir apparent, the process of landing the leading seat of authority which in most churches is still the office of the senior pastor, is quite a laborious process which varies by the context. I've personally had the chance to be examined or interviewed by at least five grueling examining committees a.k.a. "search" or "pulpit" committees. Three of them afforded me the opportunity of having my name listed on a ballot, and two accepted the will of God for me to serve as their pastor.

The process of experiencing the "candidacy" of a pulpit is an extremely time consuming and often depressing process. Many tears are shed, congregations are often divided and the journey poses challenges upon the mental, physical and even spiritual life of the preacher/candidate. Many pastors have assumed the leading seat and quickly resented their decision. For many new pastors, what was a grand first day and first few weeks quickly transitioned to a modern day Garden of Gethsemane. Many have concluded that being an associate minister was really one of the greatest roles to have had. For a traveling preacher, that "*stick,*" "*dog*" and/or two other favorite, proven sermons that characterized the sophomoric profundity and preparedness of your gift, were soon exposed and uncovered when the assignment became weekly and not just by occasion. My predecessor, Dr. Benjamin W. Robertson, Sr., in his book **Led by the Spirit,** states "…every preacher has a few sermons that they have preached so often that it becomes natural for them."

One of the greatest names to be called in addition to terms of endearment that are indicative to those of us who are married or have children is to be called "Pastor." That's an honor that should not be disregarded or disrespected by the person being identified as

"…every preacher has a few sermons that they have preached so often that it becomes natural for them."

such nor the congregations who must care for us. Without question, the respect should be reciprocal. There is such solace for a pastor to know that there are more sheep than wolves and that the "burden bearers" far outnumber those members who've resorted to being members of the "bitter bunch."

I've personally had the awesome and rewarding opportunity of serving with two dynamic congregations. While their demographics and numerical standing differ, similar personalities seem to be characteristic of them both. In other words (and I say this with love and humor), they both have had the same personalities with different names. This is certainly not an overly exaggerated summarization, but it is a truth that is really paramount for most congregations. We all pastor the same personalities and people.

It's So Hard To Say "Goodbye"

I'm thankful for my first church and the first chapter of my pastoral career. That ministry context was the conduit which prepared me for the challenges to be overcome in the future. However, seasons change, opportunities arise, assignments are completed and new quests remain on the horizon. Kenny Rogers once sang the lyrics to a song that suggested, *"If you're gonna play the game, boy, you gotta learn to play it right, you've got to know when to hold 'em, know when to fold 'em, know when to walk away, know when to run."*

I've been called an eternal optimist. But I've also had several moments when I've been extremely indecisive; one of my friends nicknamed me "Mr. Could've, Would've, Should've." Unfortunately God, unlike the mother eagle who succinctly thrusts her eaglets away from the safety and serenity of her nests, doesn't quite operate the same. He presents the opportunity and then says, "What are you going to do?"

Philanthropist and chief executive officer of Gardner Rich and Company, Mr. Chris Gardner, has one of the most remarkable journeys known. In his book, *Start Where You Are*, he writes "*So there I was in the midst of uncertainty, sitting alone in my apartment in Harlem round midnight with thunder, lightning, gunshots, and gloom all booming in the background, and I had one of those moments of altered awareness. While wondering if I should go back to hitting the anvil as I had been or do something completely different. I suddenly heard a voice from out of nowhere speak directly to me. It said only one word: "Change."*

There are many other people who've grown through major career and professional challenges in the same context with an outcome that now has them functioning in CEO and other senior level management positions. However, on the contrary, consider Oprah. When I was in my youth, I can vividly remember her as a news reporter on a local Baltimore news channel. An opportunity presented itself for her to become the host of AM Chicago, which would eventually become the Oprah Winfrey Show. Today, when I return home to Baltimore, many of the anchors/news reporters who once worked with Ms. Winfrey are still working the local channels. However, in order for Oprah to pursue her own dreams and God given destiny, a transfer was inevitable.

One could argue between either of the two career paths presented. For me, it was that of a transfer. My head had literally reached the ceiling causing a migraine and magnitude of unhealthy stress. Finances, friendships, marriage and life were all going well, but professionally I was not satisfied. I wanted to be challenged. I wanted to serve in a larger, newer arena. I honestly felt as if my personal ministry was larger than the context in which God had planted me. Observing confirmation and frustration, one of my mentors, now Bishop Dr. Dennis Proctor shared with me that "your ministry psyche is larger than your context. You are doing ministry that even my peers are not able to comprehend or implement."

One day I asked God for more.

I had a great job in Baltimore working with a wonderful group of people. There was evident job security, support and the possibility for personal, as well as professional growth.

I had a brilliant prayer request. One day I asked God for more. I felt as if my territory needed to be enlarged and that I needed to be in a place where my voice could be expanded, my name could be re-established (not that I had a bad name, almost everyone spoke well of me) and my career ambitions could be enhanced. God answered my prayers! He accepted my transfer request.

One afternoon, there was a call made to my office in Baltimore exclaiming that my resume needed to be forwarded immediately for the opportunity to pastor another church. The man who called was certainly a person of influence, but even I doubted his stance in this entire ordeal. After submitting my information, I grinned and actually remember quoting the words, "This will never happen! I'll never get that position. I'll be just a fish out of water." Was I ever so wrong? Did I ever so doubt my own resume, acumen and accomplishments? I wasn't bold enough to think differently. Subsequently, that phone call and my resume submission were really where this chapter of this blessed burden began.

Again, at the prompting and the firmness in the requestor's voice and the immediacy of the matter, my resume and biographical sketch were sent. Surprisingly, I was later told that my resume was discovered by one of the members of the Pastoral Search Committee in the garbage. It was the hand of God that led one of my now most respected deacons to discover me from amongst the trash. It was certainly the heroic and determined efforts of spirit-filled deacons that catapulted this God-ordained opportunity.

My discovery was the beginning of a process that ended up being a grueling fourteen-month journey. The journey itself could've catapulted another dissertation. During those fourteen months, my faith was tested, my future was in question and my friendships and the support I expected from familiar sources were all divested. This journey had an almost tumultuous effect on my life, because I lived life uncertain of what my future would be. Honestly, the only sustaining factor in my life was the support and love of my family, particularly my wife and children, who were happy with the life we once knew. Although they too had no idea concerning the outcome of this opportunity, they trusted my faith and relationship with God. I also remained consistent in providing for them and being the best husband and father that I could be while on the journey to this uncertain destination.

I would advise all persons considering a transition to be mindful of the pending, unpredictable and painful effects that are involved in the transfer. While the opportunity was certainly a promotion for me, my wife had to terminate employment that she loved without reservation, and my children were faced with the undesired conclusion of leaving their friends, transferring to a new school and adjusting to a totally new culture. To our chagrin, while this transfer wasn't as traumatic for my younger children, my oldest son who was entering into his first year of middle school experienced a decrease in academic achievement eventually causing my wife and me to remove him from the advanced classes to which he had initially been accepted. I'll speak concerning the effects that my family experienced in this transition in a later chapter.

The Waiting Game ~ Bloom Where You Are Planted

Uncertain of my future, I actually committed to excelling where I was while I patiently waited for the "yea" or "nay" of this inordinate opportunity that really seemed to be out of my league. At the church where I served as pastor, my commitment increased, there was evident production, growth was eminent, my character was credible, resources were available and God was still extending that grace that is so amazing. I did not have to leave, and there was a part of me that really wanted to remain. Shockingly, during the months prior to the call that would eventually conclude in a transfer, one gentleman, who was actually a "pastor's friend" and leading man within the realm of leadership told me, "Dr. Chandler, you are not going to be here long. I've got a feeling that you are going to move to another church."

I must reiterate, I did not have to leave, and the idea of me leaving, to most of my friends, foes and even my enemies, was I'm sure a thought that they never imagined would become our reality. I'm sure it was because I committed to finishing strong. I concluded that if, in fact, it would be God's plan for me to transition to another place, I was going to remain faithful to the end. A favorable response was still very uncertain for me. I observed many friends who experienced similar opportunities and with certainty they were convinced that they were a "shoe in" only to receive that phone call that even I had heard a few times before, "You didn't get enough votes." I hope that if anyone gains anything from my experience, it would be to commit to finishing strong and offering your best work and service. The reality is this, someone will win and the other will soon learn that they were not selected for the position.

There are many people who are so intrigued by an opportunity that they unintentionally or mentally divorce, resign or even retire too soon from a current occupation or way of living and are unfortunately denied the promotion or the opportunity they desired. It was the Apostle Paul who taught his younger protégé Timothy to 'remain faithful to the end.' My eventual departure I'm sure was extremely devastating to many of the people who were unfortunately "left behind." However, it is my hope that they will at least give me the credit of establishing and maintaining a credible foundation that became good soil for continued growth and productivity. It should be everyone's desire to leave a promising legacy.

As I recall the period of waiting, it was also a season of frustration. Observably, my father is a great, straight-forward speaking man. However, one trait that I inherited from him (one that we've both laughed about) is this irresistible impulse to speak before thinking. I often wonder if I am dyslexic. While revealing this personal information about myself, I'm reminded that honesty is good for the soul, but bad for a flawless image.

> *"Not all of your enemies are outside your camp. Some are inside your camp..."*
>
> — Bishop Walter S. Thomas

Well, Jesus didn't come to save the righteous, but to save the sinners. Pray for me, I'm a work in progress. Nevertheless, one of my many regrets during the wait was that I shared this possibility of a new opportunity with too many people. I later learned that often times, a promotion causes commotion.

There were many who conveyed sincerest commendations regarding the possibility of the move. Others caused me to regret ever sharing the information, because on a day when I wanted to relieve my mind of the stress of the unknown, they would be the "messengers of satan to buffet me." They would ask questions like, "have you heard anything yet? " "Are you sure you really want to do this?" "Who do you think will have your job when you're gone?"

I would warn persons to not even share the possibility of a transition with the members of even your own inner circle. While many of them are actually really excited about your elevation or promotion, the ultimate results of the transfer, unfortunately, may not involve their participation or continued and uninterrupted presence (as well as you to them) in your life without being faced with the locale challenges that may be inevitable as a result of your transfer. The reality is that your promotion may cause others to be found left behind. Unfortunately, I had people within my inner circle to intentionally create road blocks which adversely affected the joy of the journey. After a while and in retrospect, I just wanted it to be over. I wanted an answer that would allow me to have something new to think about and the release of the dreary and questionable unknown. Sleepless nights, secret interviews, background and credit checks, "secret shoppers" and much more, became my daily antagonists. Although this *answered prayer* presented so many promising opportunities, I agonized internally concerning the results, tossing around the affirmative and the doubts. To my chagrin, the agony during the waiting period, the transfer and many decisions made as a result of it, regrettably caused much friction and unnecessary grief within a once solid bond of friends, which is still difficult to overcome and even comprehend.

The Late Night Caller

I'll never forget the call that was the initial deal closer. In my process of promotion an election was held. I was recommended for the position by a vote that resulted in a very close margin. The decision was so close; it was actually about 51/49. However, the number was in my favor, but everyone knew that I only won by a very short margin. This was also a lesson in humility for me. Not only was I convinced that I was the best man for the job, but I also had everything working in my favor. I had an earned doctorate, a respectable resume, age, spirituality, personality, an awesome recommendation from people of influence, a solid family and great looks. The number of votes I received exceeded my opponent's total by a mere eleven votes.

I was pretty confident that there were a few members of the examining committee who sincerely wanted the vote to work in my favor. Obviously, there were those who in hindsight, although extremely Christian in their actions were still not convinced that I was the man for the job. It was obvious that I wasn't the choice of the person who was directed to make the call. Although very professional, the caller, as I can so vividly remember, had an extremely monotone and doleful congratulatory greeting. (You will really appreciate the role of "the caller" later. I promise.)

The call informing me that I was "the one" came approximately 9 p.m. on a Tuesday night while I was working late at my office at the church in Baltimore. Honestly, one of my beloved trustees, a little birdie I would say, had already informed me two days prior that the position was most likely mine, but that call made it official. I can still remember the somber voice of the Tuesday night caller saying, "Well, I just called to congratulate you. The congregation elected you as our new Pastor."

Appreciative, relieved and honored, I tearfully hung up the phone more afraid than I'd ever been through the entire process. I immediately drove home to embrace my wife and my oldest son (who should've been sleeping). I held them close while in the sitting area of my bedroom in the dream home that would in a few more months have a "For Sale" sign on the front lawn. Grabbing them, my wife and son tightly, I echoed these words, "We're moving to Richmond." Tearfully and joyfully, we huddled together as the Baltimore Ravens have done on so many victories (I had to throw my team in some kind of way). We all shed a few tears as they both congratulated me on my promotion. Little did I know that this was to be the beginning of many sleepless nights.

The Day I Dreaded Most

As previously stated, I had a job that I loved with complete abandon. During my seven and a half year journey, I saw a congregation of less than 50 people grow to more than 600. We had recently moved into a newly renovated administrative building and purchased several vacant lots to address our parking concerns. At my first church, I had the opportunity to eulogize loved ones, marry friends, dedicate babies, provide spiritual direction, and develop meaningful ministry and life opportunities for people of extremely diverse backgrounds. I was privileged to write and practice sermons and become a friend, as well as spiritual leader, to people who still affectionately call me "Pastor."

There was a previously planned annual meeting scheduled, unbelievably, the very next day after I received the call. I had less than 22 hours to prepare a letter of resignation informing a group of loving and supportive people, who had no idea that I had ever been courted by another congregation, that I was leaving. I couldn't even pen the words alone. I'm thankful for one of my best friends, Dr. Jamal Bryant, who met me at my office and assisted me in writing my letter of resignation. I also had my pastors, Bishop Aggie Brown, Sr., Bishop Oscar Brown and my big brother in the gospel, Dr. Aggie Brown, Jr. at the meeting. This was the document that I tearfully stood and read to the crowd in attendance:

> Noted author, Charles Dickens in his masterpiece entitled, The Tale of Two Cities, begins chapter one with this opening line... "it was the best of times; it was the worst of times!"
>
> And that's how I feel right now.
>
> For the past seven years and eight months as pastor of the New Bethlehem Baptist Church, for me every day has been Christmas and all of you have been my gifts. When I think about:
>
> ~ Our first Sunday here, with little Anthony in our arms, and Taleshia pregnant with Alysha
> ~ I remember the welcome sign and the gifts given
> ~ I remember the first gift we purchased, that Hammond Organ
> ~ I remember installing the speakers late, but early one Sunday morning
> ~ I remember the Leadership Training Classes
> ~ I saw the community inspired
> ~ You were so supportive when I completed my Doctoral Degree
> ~ I remember purchasing the properties across the street
> ~ I remember the numerous retreats and fellowships
> ~ I remember the happy times, as well as the sad times, we shared
>
> We've welcomed God's most prolific and anointed

preachers and singers, but again, it is the best of times, and it is also the worst of times!

When I was about seven years old, one Christmas morning, I woke up early and went under the tree to open my present. In my haste I received a paper cut and began to bleed, but I did not want be so engrossed by the pain, that I failed to recognize that in my hand was a present, a gift. I remembered that experience again last night. Although in my spirit, I have known that this day would come, last night I experienced what I would call the best of times, and also the worst of times.

Last night, I received a call from a Trustee of the Cedar Street Baptist Church of God in Richmond, Virginia informing me that the church had elected me to be their new pastor. Right now my whole family is emotionally bleeding because we see this as a present from God, but we are in pain. This is for us the best of times and the worst of times.

After much prayer, fasting, meditation and reflection, I had a moment like Jesus in the Garden of Gethsemane where Jesus said, "Not my will, but Thine will be done." With you on my mind, God spoke to me and said, "These are not your people, but they are my people." At His Word, I have humbly accepted the Divine opportunity to Pastor the congregation of the Cedar Street Baptist Church in Richmond, Virginia, and I will begin the first Sunday in January. While I am leaving the city, you all are never leaving my heart. There is an old R & B song that says no matter how high I get, I will still be looking up to you. So no matter where I am in the world, no matter where the Lord takes me, New Bethlehem, you taught me how to pastor, you taught me how to lead, you taught me how to preach and you taught me how to serve...I am because of you.

In closing I say this, for seven years you have showered my family with affection. For seven Christmases you have blessed our hearts with cards, seeds and gifts. Just in case any of you were trying to get me a gift for Christmas, the best gift that you can give me is to remain faithful to God and to the work that we've begun at New Bethlehem. Never second guess my love for any of you or for this church. This is not what I chose, but what God has chosen for me. This is not something that I pursued; this was something that was destined for my life.

Because this is a difficult moment for me and my family, I ask that you would keep us in your prayers knowing that we will continue to pray for you every day. I ask that you would allow us this time to begin planning for the shift that is taking place in our life. Having said that, tonight, we ask that you would comfort each other as you celebrate what God has allowed us to accomplish together. It would be too emotional for us to personally talk or share with each of you. However, I will make myself available to all of you. If you need to schedule a personal appointment with me, please feel free to call the church office tomorrow, and we will do so. I love you all, and although this is painful, I do believe, that this is the will of God for my life.

The reading of that document by far, remains one of the hardest moments and the most difficult conversation that I've ever had. With the exception of guiding friends through the loss of their deceased toddler, the reading of that letter was the most difficult moment of my pastoral career. I couldn't even complete the reading of my letter without tears flowing down my face and my voice cracking and breaking as I tried to control the sadness of looking out over the faces reflecting back to me. My wife, who never attended this annual meeting per my request, was there to stand by my side. In addition, our pastors were also present, one to encourage me, the other to encourage the congregation and who remained after I asked to be dismissed at the conclusion of reading my letter.

My mentor, Dr. William Curtis, a very successful pastor in Pittsburgh, afforded me valuable advisement that I ignored. In laymen's terms (a tone that he, the ardent Howard man he is, hardly ever speaks) he told me to "get out as fast as you can." My thoughts during that time were that of a pastor. I was really trying to act as God and serve like Jesus. Why do we make feeble attempts to be God? We can neither heal nor soothe broken hearts, only He can.

Once again I was found guilty of not listening to wise counsel. I submit to you this theory. If you've welcomed a mentor in your life, listen to the insights and wisdom being shared. On too many instances as both a minister and pastor,

I've incurred unnecessary distresses all because I failed to listen to the advice provided. *"...Oh what needless pains we bear!"*

Nevertheless, I made every attempt to continue to act as their pastor, and I thought it appropriate for me to remain to pastor the congregation through this season of grief and loss—losing the pastor who for many was their first. Mission impossible! Soon I concluded that my presence only made matters worse. My presence was like that of a husband who had recently told his wife that he was leaving for another woman, but he remained to share the same bed for a few more days. That *ain't gonna* happen on any planet. In hindsight, my advice to anyone in transition would be to get out as fast as you can.

Unfortunately, once I made the announcement, and truthfully speaking, my heart was now alive in my new opportunity. The Bible says, "For where a man's treasure is, there your heart will be also." I was making attempts to remain attached to something from which my mind and heart was now detached. As much as I loved the great people of that church, my assignment there was complete. Significantly, my moving forward was at a time when ministry there was both extraordinary and outstanding. I certainly departed (and I challenge everyone making similar transitions) to leave on a 'high-note!' Certainly their hearts were broken, but few, if any, could say that I left them worse off than they were when I arrived.

Once the news (I don't know whether it was good or bad news) was circulated throughout the congregation, and by now the entire city, it seemed like I had "six in one hand and a half dozen in the other." There was a group of people, family members and friends who joyfully celebrated my promotion, but there was another group, beloved congregants, as well as friends, who found it extremely difficult to even be in my presence. Some have still not been able to overcome the loss with my taking the new position. Gladly, because of a prescheduled Christmas presentation, I didn't have to preach the Sunday following the announcement. It was a somber recessional at the conclusion of the presentation as my soon to be former congregants would begin their journey of saying farewell.

Once the news had surfaced, I received several letters and email from members of both congregations.

> *Dr. Chandler,*
> *My husband and I are elated that you have been selected to lead our Church family. From the first time we heard you, we were very impressed and felt that you were equipped to lead us to higher levels. We look forward to working with you and your family, and we know that God intervened and made all that has happened possible. If we can be of any assistance in your transition, please call us at 804-***-*****
> *A & C*

> *Hey Pastor,*
> *Just got home and heard about your decision. I can't imagine how hard it was for you to accept. Please know you are always in my prayers, and I wish we can be closer than we were. I hope this does not mean I am losing a mentor and friend. I am true to my commitment and need to know how I handle this as a minister to the church. I wish*

I could have been there tonight. Maybe it would be easier to answer the many questions people are asking. If there is anything I can do to help the church, please let me know. As I said, I know this must be hard for you, but if you ever need someone to talk to, know that I am here. I will be up for awhile working, so call me if you need me.
Minister H.

Hey Pastor,

I just heard the news and I wanted to say congrats! I know your phone is going to be ringing off the hook, so I said I would email you. When I first heard, I felt like crying. I was happy for you, but I felt like I was losing you! I know I'm not, but you are just a little further! I know it's a little hard because of all the history you have at New Bethlehem, but when God opens a door you have to take it! Richmond & Cedar Street don't know how blessed they really are to have you there, but they will soon find out! I thank you for everything you have done in my life and ministry. I am because of you! People are saying Pastor Chandler is blessed because he is going to that big church. But I am saying, "that big church is blessed because they got Pastor Chandler!" I am proud to say that you are my Pastor!! Thank you for giving me an example to look up to! I love you!
V.S.

Good morning Pastor,
 I know you received a lot of negative responses because of God's will for your life and ministry, but I'm just sending you this e-mail to let you know I'm praying for you! Some people just don't understand that once you say "yes" to God, your life is really not your own anymore. No matter how much we want to do our own thing, in the long run, it's always God's will. I know God has a lot more in store for you. His word states, "When we're faithful over a few, He'll make us rulers over many." I PRAISE GOD FOR YOUR ELEVATION!
Rev. M. S.

Pastor Chandler,
 I just want to tell you to be encouraged! You have done great things at NBBC. I know that God has great things in store for you and your family. Wherever you go, you will be successful. Your year of completion was 2007, and your year of new beginnings is 2008. I appreciate all you have done for me and my family! Love you and your family!
Mrs. S. J.

Dr. Chandler,
 We are so excited to have you as our new pastor. We know that you will soon be looking for a new home. We welcome you and your family to stay at our home if the need arises. We know that God sent you to Cedar Street. We can't wait for

you to officially begin as our Pastor. God bless you, Mrs. Chandler and children.

R & J

I saved these letters knowing that they would one day become useful. There were so many others who provided source, strength and even served as an anchor during the transition. One memorable moment was a meeting scheduled with a gentleman who served in the band at New Bethlehem. He was extremely disappointed by my decision to leave. He joined the church as a layperson not too long after he had terminated his membership at his home church where his father served as pastor. To him, I was more than just a pastor. I had become a surrogate father to him. During our conference, he couldn't resist the tears that relentlessly fell from his eyes. I can vividly recall him asking me, "Why are you doing this?"

Those concluding moments as pastor of New Bethlehem were daunting. There were moments when I felt as if I was abandoning the congregation. Many of my dearest members refused to even say "goodbye." For them it was just too difficult. Unbeknownst to them, I agonized for months prior to receiving the "official call" offering me the job – not looking forward to the moment when I would have to inform them that I was leaving.

At the guiding of the Holy Spirit, I invited a trusted mentor and spiritual father, Bishop (Dr.) Michael Dantley, (Pastor of the Christ Emmanuel Christian Fellowship Church in Cincinnati, Ohio – one of my favorite congregations to minister) one who had established a great rapport with the congregation to serve as the guest preacher on my final Sunday there. He was absolutely phenomenal in preaching to both me and the congregation during this uneasy season of transition. This was really the first phase of healing for both me and the congregation. His sermon title was "When the Prince Leaves." There will come a time in every Pastor's life when that Pastor will need the presence, comfort and care of another Pastor. For me, that was the time.

Ironically, my last sermon preached as pastor of New Bethlehem Baptist Church in Baltimore, Maryland was watch night 2008 (December 31, 2007). I had, so I thought, a great sermon. I had energy, charisma, and a solid Word, but they sat on me and barely responded to anything that I said. I was clearly the poster child of Dr. H. Beecher Hicks' most noted book, *Preaching through a Storm*. As with past watch night services, the church was jammed for both the 7 p.m. and 10 p.m. services; but the reality was this, the church was losing their pastor.

By the conclusion of that day, most of my office had already been cleared, and I was assertively asked by one of the elders to submit my keys prior to the start of the second service. I was also informed that my recommendation to assist them in supplying the pulpit after my departure and my good intentions to help them with the preliminary work to search for a new pastor were not necessary.

Surprisingly, and with the belief that another congregation was anticipating my arrival, I believe I received this rejection during my final moments well. One chapter had closed, but another was soon to begin.

Chapter Three

The Burden Of Arrival: There's A New Kid On The Block

"When a boy comes to school without knowing his lesson, he should be studied instead of being punished."

Dr. Carter G. Woodson
The Mis-Education of the Negro

Chapter Three ~ The Burden Of Arrival: There's A New Kid On The Block

Athleticism has never been something that would be on my list of special interests. Another memory from middle school was when my family moved into an apartment on the northwest side of Baltimore. I felt like Lionel Jefferson. We were moving on up. As the new kid in the neighborhood, I was asked to participate in a simple game of touch football. Acceptance has always mattered to me and I've always been a person to try most things at least once. On that afternoon, I guess I was nine years old; I was welcomed to play football. For a few minutes, I was a humble participant in the game. However, it was now my time to run the ball. My recent observation of the game was to make sure that I avoided any contact from members of the opposing team. That's exactly what I did. However, my attempts to avoid contact and with the hopes of protecting the ball, I ignorantly ran the ball in the wrong direction. This obviously caused me to be kicked off the team and eventually out of the game. I had the ball, but I was running in the wrong direction. To make matters worse, my cheerleader mom watched this entire episode as she sat like David's wife, Micah, by the window.

Needless to say my first encounter with my new

friends wasn't an experience that won me immediate, if any, popularity. For the group who was patiently awaiting my arrival as their new pastor, this was one of the questions at hand. Will we like this new guy, our new young pastor? As fate would have it to be, I've been honored to succeed two pastors who led the congregation for more than four decades. At New Bethlehem, Dr. William Rivers, who pastored for 48 years until his death, and Dr. Benjamin W. Robertson, Sr., who pastored 52 years at Cedar Street, and transitioned just a month before I was to celebrate my third anniversary as pastor of the Cedar Street Church. Dr. William Curtis admonishes that I've been gifted to transition somewhat traditional churches into contemporary, progressive ones. However, at both of my arrivals at the churches I've been called to serve, the storm always preceded the calm.

As with most new pastors or persons who are now occupying the title and/or seat of someone who has been loved, respected, and admired, the pressure of the new individual is heightened. This should be expected. Most people have a genuine respect and reverence for their pastor. At least hopefully, there is respect. The pastor is the individual sent from God, so we believe, who prepares, challenges and creates the spiritual momentum of being. He or she should be one who preaches, teaches and lives according to Biblical precepts, but he should also have personality and influence and be approachable. I had all of these characteristics, but lacked wisdom in the beginning, which facilitated a plethora of letters, emails, dismissals and a few church transfers. In the words of one of my favorite singers, John Legend, I would encourage all new pastors to "take it slow!"

Great Ideas, Bad Timing

Change is necessary. Change is inevitable. However, change must also at times be communicated, evaluated, and sometimes patiently awaited. As one of the most sagacious saints of my congregation once shared with me, "It's an awfully poor wind if it doesn't change some time."

What appeared to be wrong to me was actually right for everyone else. What appears to be great to many is good, average or even awful to others. As I reflect on many of the changes implemented in my first years of pastoring, I still wonder how I was able to successfully demonstrate my misconstrued powers in such a way to get away with them. Bishop Andrew Turner, another trusted father and renowned preacher in Los Angeles would call it this: **GRACE!**

In retrospect, many of the changes, which should actually be considered transitioning, were both necessary and warranted. Once most people accepted the rationale, they could more effectively and consciously adapt to the change. Subsequently, it wasn't the senior's circle, those members 60 and above, who created challenges in embracing the change. It was the 40 to late 50's crowd who very assertively asked, "What in the hell is he doing?"

The response of the seasoned saints was this, "He'll learn."

I would advise all new pastors to love on, embrace, listen to and even visit the seasoned saints. There were many battles that I did not have to fight because my seasoned saints had my back. They also make some great sweet potato pies and are always spoiling my family. For many of the seasoned saints in both of the congregations that I've been honored to serve, they were actively involved in ministry upon the arrival and even early years of my predecessors. Many of them would share with me these same words, "Everything that you are being confronted with, Reverend (speaking of the former pastors) had to endure the same. Hang on in there. Keep God first, and He will see you through."

Many of the members who were just around my mother's age had difficulty with my early decisions. I later learned that for many of them, they had children who are my age. What at first seemed to be opposition, was really (for a few) just concern and protective instincts that generated sincere concern about both the good of the church, as well as their new pastor. There are people within the congregation who, as sad as it seems, really have been agents, anointed by demonic forces to destroy God's chosen vessel and to cause havoc within the camp. On the contrary, I believe that the majority really want to see the pastor and the church thrive and maintain Biblical transformation. However, for many new pastors, much effort is spent warring with the minority, so that the majority is left asking this question, "When will the pastor focus on the supporters and not on the naysayers who are *loving* the attention being administered from the pulpit."

The ones, who support you in the beginning, quickly turn against you!

For most new pastors, there is a group who has been waiting for your arrival. There is a group who desires to be the pastor's advisors or circle, or using a more familiar term, they want to be in the clique. Upon my arrival at both churches, obviously, these people as Clint Eastwood would say *they make your day!* People of irrelevance need people of relevance to validate their person. As a new pastor, friendships, acceptance and support are certainly tools to be desired. However, in the words of Jesus, "I am sending you out like sheep among wolves. Therefore be as shrewd as snakes and as innocent as doves." (Matthew 10:16 NIV)

While there have been many consistent people who've remained immutable throughout my journey as pastor, there have been others who've flipped the script and have changed from the kindhearted, gentle David Bruce Banner into that ugly, green monster known as the Incredible Hulk. What I've discovered on my journey as pastor is to always search for men and women who possess heart more than skill and/or even personality. Many of my greatest disappointments have been birthed out of my inability to decipher and detect the motives of some of the people around me.

Never Trust A Big Hug And A Smile

One would argue that even Jesus was betrayed by Judas. That's a Biblical fact. Subsequently, I really don't believe that Judas, when originally selected, could have been characterized or even considered a threat to Jesus or His ministry. As with all of us, people make choices. By nature, I believe that all people are good. However, even the greatest and most saintly among us, must contend with the un-benefited effects that often is the plot of our days.

By my very nature, I am a lover of people. I've always been the one (even in my early youth) who could have easily and hands down been voted Mr. Compassionate. I was the one who supplied tissue for the kid in the class who always had a runny nose. I was the one who ate lunch with the classmate who others classified as the "pig pen" of the crowd. As an adult, I've also been the person who's been the greatest supporter of the underdog, the castaway and the rejected. My wife describes this as a "cloudy heart", because I have a soft spot and genuine compassion for other people.

However, ministry has taught me something valuable: Guard your heart at all times. One of my elder brothers in ministry, Dr. Dante Hickman (pastor of the Southern Baptist Church in Baltimore) once told me, "Chandler, never trust anyone!"

Of course, no matter how well you guard your heart, it will be broken. Also, living life with an inability to trust anyone won't take you very far. As the new kid on the block, you must just take it slow. Everyone is not against you, just as everyone is not for you. Time will tell. There are people who are like locusts. They will irritate the hell out of you with an attempt to jump on your being and, just like ticks, they go for blood. The good news is that insects, for the most part, are only seasonal. You must commit to tolerating their existence for a season, overload yourself with as much Biblical fumigation as possible and try your best to refrain from running away or killing the butterflies and birds in the process. Many pastors declare war with rage against the naysayers, but they damage the supporters in the process. I don't know of too many new pastors who've been able to avoid this dubious duty of dealing with the "others," but this must be one of the first lessons or words of advice shared with these new servant leaders: *DON'T USE THE PULPIT TO FIGHT YOUR BATTLES!*

Never Acknowledge Anonymous Letters!

Anonymous letters forwarded:

"Dr. Chandler, I know you really love your wife, but do you have to talk about her and acknowledge her every Sunday. My family and I would appreciate it, if you did not acknowledge her as much."

"Dr. Chandler, Your sermons are extremely hurtful to

people. Why do you expect everyone to jump and shout when you preach? Also, the music is too loud. Why do we have dancers? That is totally a waste of time. I've been a member of this church for over 50 years. We've built this church and you are not going to tear it apart.

*Also the minutes (*I think this person meant the announcements) *shouldn't be played over the intercom. You are making too many changes. Give us a break!"*

I remember during the early days of my second pastorate, there was an awful emergence of rumors, scheming and a strategy to remove me from the pulpit. Unbeknownst to me at that time, this was a group of cowards who

> "There's a war going on between those who want God and those who don't want God. Like it or not, you are involved."

for lack of more mature words, were just a group of inactive and now disconnected church members, who seemed to have a problem with everything. I would later name this group of immature adults, "the bitter bunch." I've also learned that every pastor and/or person of influence has to contend with the "bitter bunch." Their timing was perfect. Their plotting and scheming in addition to the stratagem pursued to remove me, was while I was on vacation. Matter of fact, what I've noticed as a pastor is that it's similar to an old adage that I learned watching Tom and Jerry, "When the cat is away, the mouse will play."

It was perfect timing to say the least. Yes, I was on vacation, but it was also a time when my wife was scheduled to have surgery. While praying and believing God for a successful surgery patiently waiting in the family room of a Baltimore hospital, I received a phone call that informed me that there was a petition to remove me as Pastor. Talk about being caught between a rock and a hard place. I was miles away from the office, my supporters, and my new church family who overwhelmingly displayed expressions of love toward me and my family. The person I love most, my best friend, wife and life companion was now under the knife. I was so overwhelmed with emotion that I left the hospital and cried in my car. I couldn't believe that this was happening to me.

The Sunday following vacation ended with my wife's surgery and the long, slow ride back to Richmond (because she was still sore from her surgery). In my mind, I was returning to war. I had all of the right West Baltimore words to say. I had my ammunition and was armed and dangerous. I can remember this experience as if it was yesterday.

As I was preparing for the service, one of the many great deacons of my congregation, Deacon Willie Brown, Sr., came to my office just before the start of the service and asked all of those persons in my office to step out. He then walked the stairs of my office and spoke to me with love as a deacon, father and Christian and said to me, "Pastor, today we need a Word! Today, I need you to preach Jesus."

His words on that July Sunday morning were as if God Himself was speaking to me. He firmly embraced me with love, prayed for me and on that Sunday, I preached one of the best sermons I've ever preached in my life. My supporters were evident and to my surprise, eighty percent of the people had no idea that any of that buffoonery was taking place.

New pastors and my brothers and sisters of this calling, our mandate, mission and assignment is to preach that Jesus Christ is Lord and that He reigns and is still on the throne. To those persons of other occupations, remember that your assignment is larger than the adversaries among you. Our adversaries are simply present as the conduits that advance the opportunity, work and passion of our call.

Your Naysayers Become Supporters

In the Book of Acts, one of the meanest and most obstinate characters on the scene was a young scholar by the name of Saul. He was an individual who Eugene Peterson, the author of *The Message*, declared as being a person who was wreaking havoc on the church or as theologians would identify as the "people of the Way." However, a detailed look and study of Saul's journey would later inform us that Saul would become the greatest soul winner created by God. My friends, God can change the hearts of enemies, naysayers and adversaries to become your greatest allies.

Earlier in this book, I spoke concerning "the caller," or if you are just picking up this book, the person who was designated to inform me that I was chosen to serve as their new pastor. Initially, "The caller" by virtue of the tone and tenor of her voice when the call was made, was not a happy camper. I was not her choice, and she later informed me of her vote against me and the reasons why. "The caller" as I've been told, was one of the greatest cheerleaders of the other candidate considered for the position. Just as there were persons influencing the decision of the crowd to vote in my favor, she was doing the exact same for her candidate.

However, and this is another moment in ministry that is vividly remembered, on my first Sunday as pastor, I don't know how this happened, but "the caller" was the person on the program to present welcoming gifts to me and my family and was also one of the persons responsible for the grand chitterling dinner which followed the morning service. On that Sunday as "the caller" presented gifts, she sincerely, truthfully and with a microphone in her hand told me that I was her pastor and that we/she was going to do everything in her power to take care of me and my family. Of course, my "cheerleaders" and supporters were just as flabbergasted as I was. I remember seeing the concerned looks and even hearing a few purrs.

Actions Speak Louder Than Words

Adjusting to the wonderful southern climate was not an easy task for a person from the urban metropolis of Baltimore City. My bronchial and seasonal coughing challenges became very difficult in my first month of relocating to Richmond. My wife, caregiver and now weekend partner remained in Baltimore to maintain our home matters and worked diligently as a special educator in the Baltimore City School System while remaining both supermom and dad status at home. I had no family to reach out to in Richmond. There were many among my new church family who displayed notable care and concern for me, but I was still the new kid on the block. It was then that "the caller" was viewed as not just a talker, but a doer. Concerned, worried and observant of my discomfort, she became the friend, mother and Christian that she so succinctly committed to being on my first Sunday as pastor.

For the sake of being accused of building this chapter writing about "the caller," I just want to admonish and advise the "new kids" to never underestimate the power and ability of God to change people. "The caller" is now one of my leading supporters. Again, people are not bad. They are human. Instead of joining my supporters in warring with members of the "other side," I chose to live a life that was pleasing to God, conduct myself in a manner that was indicative of my title and role and to love the hell out of people. I committed to Matthew 5:16.

Display Love At All Times

As the "new kid," all eyes are on you. There were times and still are moments, when I feel as if I'm being followed. Of course and as previously stated, with almost any position, there is a convergence of people who've already counted you out, underestimated your skills and abilities and have already numbered your days. There was a public statement overheard by many in the city of Richmond that I wouldn't last for one year as the pastor of the church that I've served now for four years. One of my favorite mantras is "you can catch more bees with honey than vinegar."

My pastor and father in ministry, Bishop Aggie Brown, Sr., the pastor emeritus of the Great Dalton Church in Baltimore, epitomized this characteristic during thirty plus years of pastoring. There were times when he was acquiescently disrespected, but his response after almost every memorable encounter was always characterized with compassion. He never seemed to remain angry with anyone. He has mastered the ability to "shake it off and pack it under your feet."

What many people in my position and other CEOs or leading positions fail to display is personality. Many CEOs and pastors have personalities that suck. They are always busy and unapproachable, often overly polished and postured and many times more consumed with rock star status, failing to be a servant of all. I agree with the person who said that congregations have the DNA of their pastor. The problem is this – too many pastors don't have the DNA of God. Arrogance, personal advancement, and disingenuous attitudes have eroded the sacred desks of ministry and too many of us have failed at the art of being a servant. The pastor must be able to connect with the people. Dr. Ann Lightner-Fuller, my spiritual mother and pastor of the Mt. Calvary AME Church in Towson, Maryland once told me, "You build a people, you build a church."

Personality matters. I also know and understand that with most persons occupying a role of leadership, we are often expected to become all things to and for all people. One response would be, "To whom much is given, much is expected." Just suck it up and do what is expected. However, for many, that's easier said than done. Nevertheless with most people, the first step in diminishing or de-escalating a potentially explosive relationship or situation is simply learning their name.

In the Book of Job chapter one, an unlikely and uninvited visitor attended the worship in progress in Heaven. As the devil appeared on the scene, God didn't identify his presence by virtue of his character. He called the devil by his name and said, "Satan, why are you here?" Now on the contrary, on many occasions when we are visited by those among us, who make committed attempts to ruin our life and journey, we are often tempted to expressively call, talk and even engage them by saying, "Good day, Satan, how are you today?"

Of course, that would make most of our days, but would it further the cause of Christ? We must resist the urge of communicating to the enemy within a person and acknowledge that their external portrayal could possibly be totally opposite to their internal being. With most people, their bark is greater than their bite and a simple gesture of learning and getting to know a person's name could be a critical step in winning that person.

I'm Staying And You Are Going To Love Me

At times, being the new kid on the block is difficult. Not just as a new pastor, but as a new leader in the town. There were many locals who desperately wanted to occupy my seat. There were numerous wagers out on me and many didn't believe I'd survive one year. I was the fast paced, Baltimore-enunciating preacher from up north now serving a traditional, respected congregation in the Commonwealth of Virginia. Although a very church oriented town, there were many negative comments heard and shared from members of the religious community about the new pastor in town. A non-member of my congregation even had a fresh copy of the contract presented to me by the search committee.

In the first months of my new pastorate, there were numerous unsigned, angry letters forwarded to my office, threats over my life, multiple questions concerning my past involvement with church conventions (Full Gospel) and conversations surrounding my acceptance of another pastoral opportunity. I don't recall any planned attacks or criticisms regarding my family. Although I am not oblivious to the idea or reality that there were "eyes" on my family, I am also convinced that my new congregation understood that attacking me was tolerable, but to attack my family was totally off limits. My alter ego reflects the character of James Evans from *Good Times* and the role that Rockmond Dunbar (my favorite actor) portrayed as Kenny in *Soul Food*. I'm a preacher, but I'm not all the way there yet!

Despite the rumors, innuendos, stares and ungodly gestures observed by a few members of what I would like to again acknowledge as the "bitter bunch," I was encouraged by the words of my mother-in-love, the right Evangelist-

Prophetess Judith Pearson who 'learned' me something several years ago. She said, "Anthony, God will not judge you by how people treat you, but He will judge you by how you treat other people."

That saying has become a personal mantra for me. Regardless of what others have spoken or done, I chose to love. I would encourage all new kids on the block to counteract the *Sad-U-cees* in your life the same. In both of

> "Where folk are fickle, God is faithful."

my pastorates, profane words have been uttered against me, invitations to meet outside have been offered and countless other invitations that if shared, would have an adverse effect on the church. I'll plead the fifth on that.

Here is something that I also discovered. The majority, the supporters, are also watching how the new kid responds. There were even some who I would call the borderline, lukewarm supporters. They weren't really in my corner, but they were not totally against me. When the new leader responds to negative situations and people with wisdom, respect and maturity, others will be won. I once heard Dr. Jeremiah Wright, the Pastor Emeritus of the Trinity United Church of Christ in Chicago say, "Where folk are fickle, God is faithful."

There is no avoidance of mistakes, errors and/or downright stupid decisions. These are all products that produce great leaders, especially great pastors. I've had more "dumb days" than I care to share. As I reflect upon this journey, there have been too many occasions when I've asked, "What in the hell was I thinking?"

If it is God's will and your intent to remain and be successful, here are some simple lessons learned that I

willingly want to share:
- Everyone who is by your side is not necessarily in your corner.
- Most people who start with you won't finish. Just because someone worked well where you were, that doesn't mean that they will work well where you are.
- Don't become too friendly. You are the pastor, not a friend.
- There are two Biblical offices in the church. Don't frustrate yourself with the additions created by man.

  "If you've got to break down, break down in front of God and not in front of people."

- If you're in a meeting and you feel the tears welling or begin seeing your skin turning green, excuse yourself and go to the bathroom. Regain your composure and return to the meeting.

- If you are communicating words searched by way of the thesaurus or internet, learn the proper pronunciation of the word or phrase before you use it. Ignorance is bliss.

- The church hired you, not your spouse. Allow your spouse to serve when and where comfortable and not because they are the preacher's wife/husband.

- If a person can commit as a volunteer, they'll be a heck of an employee.

- Every opportunity is not necessarily a blessing.

- Don't fire the inherited staff upon arrival. Work with them. They may become your most faithful allies and trusted friends.

- Get to know your leaders. It's a sad general who doesn't know his soldiers.

- Pray for a mentor you trust and listen!

- You don't always get what you deserve, you get what you negotiate.

- If you can't do it for all, don't do it for one.

- Join a gym. You need a place and a day to release your frustrations. The Sabbath is not just a day of worship; it's a day of rest. Make a Sabbath beyond the Sabbath Day.

- Only invite people into your home if you are convinced that they can handle your prosperity, home drama and you with your socks off.

> *I am eternally grateful for the many family members gained during my tenure as pastor.*

- Allow your spouse and children the time to choose their own friends. They can detect a hypocrite more effectively than you.

- Adopt a mother, father, sister and/or brother. These are people who will tell you the truth, hold your hand, fight for you and love you no matter how many wrong moves you make. (I am eternally grateful for the many family members gained during my tenure as pastor.)

- Just because someone doesn't speak that doesn't mean that they are your adversary. They are just checking you out. They really do like you.

- Get to know the new members. You have something in common with them. Listen to what they say about others. Remember, everyone is not saying the same lie.

- Act like the CEO at all times!

- Work hard, play hard! Get away when you can. Hurry back. The people want to hear their pastor and not another preacher or associate minister...*no matter how good that other preacher is.*

- A great preacher doesn't necessarily make a great pastor, but a great pastor is a great preacher...he or she knows the sheep.

- Let the people see you live, love and laugh. Don't take yourself so seriously. Your members want you to have fun.

- Watch what you say and do when away from the church or office. Everybody has a family member or friend who doesn't attend your church.

- Don't ever, under any circumstances, deny or decline a person's resignation. You'll regret it one day later.

- Don't forget your old friends. They may be your only friends. New cities are not always hospitable to new people. You may be fortunate enough to find one, but most of your friends will most likely live miles away from your new context.

- Maya Angelou said, "When someone shows you who they are, believe them."

- Journal your journey. You have a story that can make an easier road for someone else.

- Pray, Pray, Pray!!!!!

Always remember this, *"each victory will help, some other to win!"*

Chapter Four

The Burden To Follow: Honoring Your Predecessor

"The dead speak through the acts performed while they lived among us."

An excerpt from the book entitled *Led by the Spirit of God*
Written by Dr. Benjamin W. Robertson, Sr. (1931-2011)
The 9th Pastor of the Cedar Street Baptist Church of God
Founder, Richmond Virginia Seminary

Chapter Four ~ The Burden To Follow: Honoring Your Predecessor

An area where many new leaders fail miserably is at honoring the persons who occupied the seats we now occupy. No matter how rewarding, remarkable or ruining their tenure or time of leadership was for them, we do ourselves a great injustice in our failure to honor, commend and value their position in our transformation as successor.

In both of my pastorates, I've had the honor of succeeding two pastors who had on their resumes more than a half century of serving in the role in which I would later occupy. In my first role as pastor, Rev. William Rivers served the congregation of New Bethlehem for 48 years and Dr. Benjamin W. Robertson, Sr., pastored Cedar Street for 52 years. Without discussion, both of these men were stellar leaders, builders and national preachers who've earned the respect of thousands. Both men successfully built and paid the mortgages for sanctuaries that were cutting edge and historic in their time. For many of the people that I've served as pastor, the former pastor was the only person that they've known as their pastor. Many of my most active members were either dedicated as babies, baptized as children, married and/or have certainly welcomed my predecessors into their homes, hearts and lives as a result of the many sacerdotal duties that each of these men have responded to during their term and in the office of pastor.

Dr. William Curtis, my preaching mentor for years now, recently communicated to me that one of the qualities or characteristics that he has observed in my ministry is my uncanny, unique and sometimes unnatural ability to transform traditional congregations led by preaching and pastoring pioneers. I call it being "blessed with a burden." Whether this is my call or an inherited ability, occupying the seat of a sage and stellar leader poses more challenges than were ever discussed or introduced in seminary.

Often times, when the new pastor or CEO arrives, the urge to win support is often through the vehicle of attacking the flaws and failures of the former leader. For many newcomers, the welcoming statement or greeting of many (of course with the intent to win the newcomer) is often communicated with statements like "it's time for a change," "he/she never allowed us to do this or do it this way," "Reverend was mean, insecure, stole money." I could go on and on for pages about what I've heard people say concerning their former "Reverend."

However, in the case of my current predecessor, who God called home in February 2011, there were many people who weren't always kind in expressing words about him. However, whenever he arrived on the scene, I often wondered if those people were bi-polar or masked men and women who had disguised their true feelings and character. What I later concluded was that no matter how receptive a group or congregation appears to be concerning the arrival of their new leader, the role and contribution of the former leader in their development can never be forgotten or ignored.

Having no idea that I would serve as the pastor of New Bethlehem Baptist Church, but because of the relationship that my pastor and home church had with the church, I attended the home-going service of Dr. William Rivers. As the pastor of Cedar Street Baptist Church, with the permission of the former first lady, Dr. Dolores Robertson, and with the support of the church's leadership and congregation, I was the conductor/overseer of the home-going services of Dr. Benjamin Robertson, Sr. What I quickly observed and noted at both celebrations, the latter being the most memorable, was that the same people who were the most consistent in their murmuring against him were some of the loudest and most resolute mourners during the proceedings. It was at times, unbelievable. In my mind I was thinking, weren't you the one…?

Nevertheless and most honorably as I reflect on the role I shared in celebrating the tenure and life of Dr. Robertson, I could not in any manner as his successor, negate or overlook his role in preparing the congregation for my assignment as their new pastor. Matter of fact, on his last Sunday as pastor and during his last sermon, he admonished the congregation to work and support their new pastor. Notably on my first Sunday as the new pastor, he even shared with me as the congregation overheard these words, "This congregation is led by the pastor. If you give your authority away, well…"

He actually never completed that statement. The majority of us got the point.

As his successor, I honored him as best as I could. There was a financial arrangement already in order to care for him and his wife. Unbelievably, at one of my first meetings with my leaders, there was a very small remnant who wanted me to reverse the arrangement and terminate the agreement made prior to my arrival. As a person and especially as a pastor, I always handle, respond and even care for people as I would want them to care for me. I rejected that appeal and later recommended that we would do even more to honor him for his years of service. That additional offer awarded, by the way, was later rejected by Dr. Robertson because he did not agree with the terms.

As the new pastor or leader, especially if your predecessor is still in the "land of the living," make every attempt to honor and respect him regardless of the reason or consequence of their departure. No matter the circumstances, never publicly dishonor, speak negative words or condemn any aspect of their time, tenure or turn as the leader. If there were ever negative words parted from my lips, it was during "pillow talk" with my wife.

Remember, people are people. I'm convinced that my predecessor heard just as many rumors, comments or negative words that were supposedly communicated by me just as much as I heard the same regarding words that he was recorded of saying of me. There were moments when I was certain that he was not in agreement with my decisions or motivation to move the congregation in ways unfamiliar to him. We always remained cordial in our communication. However, there was never a public moment when there was evident disagreement or malice displayed between us. When he would occasionally *"arrive on the scene,"* I made certain that we consistently honored and acknowledged his presence. I even personally bestowed upon him the title of the "Bishop of Cedar Street."

I must share with you that in the case of Dr. Robertson, I can only recall two Sundays during his years of serving as the emeritus pastor when he was present during Sunday worship. They were my first Sunday as the new Pastor as he passed the gavel of leadership and the services on the Sunday of the official installation. To the displeasure of others, there were several comments made concerning his absence and lack of support toward me and the congregation. Many people wondered and even said, "Why doesn't he ever come to the church?"

However, I think Dr. Robertson should be commended as should this message be shared with retired pastors. The presence of the former pastor can often become a great distraction to the current one. For many congregations, as long as the former pastor or leader remains both visible and vocal, the journey of earning and gaining the respect of the crowd for the newcomer is lengthened and potentially never honored as a result of the presence and existence of the latter leader. My predecessor should be applauded for staying away; thereby giving me the space to now serve in the capacity in which God afforded him to successfully serve for 52 years.

Of the many correspondences received, this was one of my favorite emails received from Dr. Robertson in December 2008:

> *Pastor Chandler,*
>
> *It was a pleasant experience to have seen you and your family yesterday at Red Lobster. Sugar and I are happy to have such a fine looking First Family at Cedar Street. I understand that ---- is no longer in charge of the Television Ministry. I asked her to let you know that I am still interested in my museum. I do not see how those old tapes that were used during a former administration can be used when the present administration has continuation of that ministry. I would like the*

tapes for my museum. I have a garage here where I have many things ready for the museum. By the way, the TV Musical on Christmas was very good. Keep up the good work.
Benjamin W. Robertson

Working With Your Successor

If I could offer words of advice to retired and emeritus pastors or leaders, and as I remember my brief experience of working with my predecessor, I would suggest that you consider the following:

1.   You were once where that person is:

Please don't ever forget that the person who now has your seat had to start in the same position you occupied. For any newcomer, especially if the person you are now following was successful and stalwart during their term, this can be an extremely intimidating time for them. There are "big shoes" that the newcomer must now walk in. As a person who has certainly been where the "newcomer" now is, share as much as you can as soon as you can. It is my hope that the newcomer will listen.

Prior to my arrival, I remember being invited to breakfast by Dr. Robertson at the Jefferson Hotel in Richmond. What I also remember during our breakfast was how respected and how well known he was among the hotel staff and the other guests in the restaurant. Everyone knew him, and he acted as if he knew everyone. During our time of dining, he shared lessons, offered advice and made recommendations that I was able to listen and respond to accordingly. Sadly, that was the only arranged gathering we shared together while he was alive with the exception of the banquets, programs and other engagements that we just happened to share.

I believe that Dr. Robertson remembered his early days as pastor. He also knew that it would take me a moment to become acclimated with this new culture. For the most part, he remained a silent supporter of me. There were obvious periods of resistance to the many changes (I would rather identify them as transitions) that would raise real concerns. I was half his age and without argument a new age thinker from the north. Many of the traditions and customs that were exemplary during his time as pastor were certainly either outdated or representative of those pastors of his generation and not of mine. Although he was not always in total agreement, he couldn't ignore the fact that the life and enthusiasm that he once experienced as pastor had returned to the church and that the moves of the new pastor were actually moving the church forward.

2. **Stop answering and acknowledging the calls from the "bitter bunch"**

As a former pastor of a great congregation, I've also been inundated by calls, concerns and even comments shared by the person who would become my successor. I must admit it was affirming to know that a congregation that I was accused of leaving high and dry actually missed my presence and without reservation shared with me concerning their dislike or disapproval of their new leader. However, after a very brief period of entertaining the calls of a few unhappy people who in all honesty really appreciated their new leader (who in my opinion had the character, experience and leadership that would cultivate and create a plethora of change and new direction beyond my influence). They were just experiencing separation anxiety from me. I also understood that I'd been where the new pastor now is and that the new pastor of my former congregation deserved every right to create her own platform and ministerial plan. It was my duty to ignore the calls from that remnant of former congregants and concentrate on my current context.

3. Assist and speak up when necessary

As the new pastor of a very mature congregation, our sick list and bereavement ministry opportunities were often more than I could handle alone. On many occasions, once death had smitten a family, the request for "Doc" was the desire of the family. If I could share a word to the members of a congregation where the former pastor is still alive, in my opinion, the request for the former pastor to eulogize an individual shouldn't pose any threat or ill feeling to the newcomer. In my opinion, this was an honor and an opportunity for me to rest and hear another powerful sermon from such a sage "pulpiteer." Also, on many occasions, the deceased person was most often a person who I never had the opportunity of really knowing. However, "Doc" when sharing words on the deceased person's behalf, could profoundly and genuinely celebrate that person's life because of their relationship.

On the contrary, I've never returned to my former congregation to perform any pastoral duties. The difference is this. When I resigned as pastor of NBBC, I resigned to become the pastor of another congregation. I resigned because I was moving on.

In my opinion, for me to return to preside over the ceremony of a former member was a display of tremendous disrespect to the current leader. Subsequently, Dr. Robertson, when he retired, was honored and bestowed the title of pastor emeritus, which gave him the respect of his years, without the responsibilities of the title he once occupied. With my full support, Dr. Robertson returned to preach numerous funerals and, to my knowledge, he never requested any compensation. For him this became an act of love and an opportunity for him to utilize and rekindle his preaching prowess.

In retrospect, there were other times when I felt as if I really needed his assistance in communicating my vision or intentions to the congregation. I was certain that if he could only communicate his approval or support, the members of the "bitter bunch" would quickly support and commit to my plan. Consequently, what I later discovered was that many members of the "bitter bunch" were also people who he would've identified as the same. In my earlier years, the renovation of the sanctuary was not just a desire of this new pastor, it was a necessity. The reality of raising money was more than a notion. I was absolutely sure that if "Doc" were to just come by on one Sunday morning, he would have convinced the congregation to support this newcomer and would assist in expediting the process. To my chagrin, this never happened. However, the renovation process was completed and paid in full.

As his fate would have it be, at the last funeral that he was asked to preach at Cedar Street in January of 2011, "Doc" stood in the pulpit and on this visit he didn't make any jokes concerning him looking better than I. He didn't make any statements about him having more hair than I had. However, from the pulpit of the Cedar Street Church, "Doc" shared these words:

"Every time I come to Cedar Street, I see something

new and something different. This pastor has been busy. I think he's doing a fine job."

Dr. Robertson is now resting with the other preaching legends. I have regrets because I wasn't more assertive in reaching out to him. We never sat down or had the chance to break bread together since January of 2008. I respected him more than he ever probably realized. However, there is still a list of questions that I wish I had asked him.

- How did you grow Cedar Street in becoming one of the largest "black" churches in the state?
- How did you create a group of leaders with such supportive and servant-like characteristics?
- How were you able to grow a congregation while organizing your own seminary?
- How were you able to balance membership in multiple national organizations?
- What did it mean to you to serve as a founder of the Progressive National Baptist Convention?
- How were you able to preach and continue to lead with such fervor even after the untimely death of your only son?
- How did you remain a healthy pastor for 52 years?
- What were your greatest challenges, apprehensions or trepidations as pastor of CSBC?

I admonish newcomers to never have to live with the regrets that I now have as the new pastor. Get to know your predecessor. Write letters. Send emails. Be more aggressive in developing a connection. Many would say that I did the best I could in honoring "Doc." Others say that they really believe I went out of my way and often beyond the call of duty to honor his existence. In my estimation, I didn't do enough.

In a conversation with my colleague, Rev. Otis Moss, III, we reflected on the blessing of succeeding such great men. "Learning the story of the congregation through your predecessor's eyes and discovering all the family and extended family connections of a church for a new pastor are important!" stated Moss. Dr. Moss said that he learned a great deal from Dr. Jeremiah Wright, his predecessor and former pastor of the Trinity United Church of Christ in Chicago, Illinois. When asked what he would have done differently during the initial months of his pastorate at Trinity, he shared the following:

"I would have taken more time out to map out transitional strategies before Dr. Wright retired (e.g. boards, staffing, etc.). People in every church are hired because of skill, relationship or as benevolence. Learning the aforementioned practices clearly before a pastor transitions is critical to staffing in addition to other changes indicative of a new administration. Institutions have mythical memory and romanticized remembrance. The pastor must be able communicate an accurate narrative about church history, staffing changes and transitions."

Working With Your Predecessor

As previously stated, I now live with many regrets concerning my inability to establish a more congenial relationship with my predecessor. To my credit, attempts were made to establish a better relationship. By no means were we enemies. He had to have been proud of the growth, name recognition and the positive influence that I was able to cultivate and sustain concerning the church. There are a few recommendations that I would like to share with new pastors in an effort to build a better relationship with your predecessor:

1. **Be hospitable no matter the costs; save them a seat.**

Whenever your predecessor enters the building, quickly make an attempt to make them comfortable. During my entire first year as pastor of Cedar Street, there was a reserved parking space for "Doc." Due to my growing staff and his lack of attendance, after one year, his parking space was reassigned. However, whenever he would come to the church, special accommodations were arranged for his comfort. I reflect on the words of Dr. William Watley (pastor of the St. Philip AME Church in Atlanta, GA) who once told me concerning other relationships, "Maintain a loving closeness, but a healthy distance."

"Maintain a loving closeness and healthy distance."

When your predecessor arrives, unless they are comfortable remaining behind the scenes, do everything in your power to appreciate and acknowledge their presence. It will also gain you the love and support of your predecessor's ambassadors. If there is a widow/widower, honor her or him. The stress that pastor's spouses endure is unfathomable. Many clergy spouses are often uncared for and disregarded immediately following the death of the pastor. It is imperative that pastors make the necessary financial arrangements to provide security and support postmortem.

2. **Never devalue their work and accomplishments**

Whenever the history of the church is on display or read, include their work and accomplishments. You lose no honor by honoring their work. Neither erase nor devalue their sacrifices and endeavors. Remember, you will one day walk in their shoes. No one wants to be or feel forgotten. Permit a picture to hang in their honor. Remember, there are more people who know him/her than those who know you. You can't erase your predecessor's years of service. That service is now history which has paved the route for your tenure.

3. **Build on their successes and avoid making their same mistakes.**

Every noted, great leader is known for something. Discover what your predecessor was successful in accomplishing. What was the individual able to do well and how were they able to do it?

During one of our early church gatherings, I was afforded a lesson from another one of the great deacons of my church. As I sat on the dais patiently waiting for everyone in the room to be served their meal at this annual banquet, my deacon, Deacon Leo Scott, shared in my ears the following statement. He said, "At every event, "Doc" would walk around the room and greet every table." He then whispered these words, "I'm not telling you what to do. I'm just saying."

"People enjoy the touch of their pastor."

For some reason, this friendly gesture worked for Dr. Robertson. Without reservation, this same gesture is now working for me. People enjoy that touch of their pastor.

In addition to advancing your platform while building on your predecessor's strengths, avoid falling into or surrendering to their same pitfalls. I can only speak of my own failings as a pastor. During my pastorate, one of the growth curves that I wasn't able to master was my ability to concentrate more on being a pastor and not being everybody's best friend. I'm assured that this was one of the challenges of my successor who had to contend with the comments of an extremely attached congregation who wondered why our new pastor doesn't communicate with us as did our former.

I could list many more mistakes or pitfalls that I've encountered and experienced as pastor. However, I choose not to share them all because the truth does set you free, but it can also get you fired.

4. Get to know their friends.

Be well assured, your predecessor has many friends who are curious to know how you will handle your new assignment. While brown-nosing should never be the aim of anyone, respect and esteem of your predecessor's friends will further your resolve and success as the newcomer.

> *Your predecessor's enemies could very well become your supporters.*

What I've also experienced is that many times your predecessor's friends will be able to communicate to your predecessor your stance and position often times better than you can. Not just in this instance, but in a larger venue, it's a wonderful feeling to see your adversary's friends fighting on your behalf.

5. Don't make their enemies your enemies.

Without further discussion, every leader has vehemently venomous enemies. It doesn't matter how great a person is there is somebody who doesn't acknowledge or appreciate their greatness. However, don't fall into the trap of building your enemy base while adding someone else's. Your predecessor's enemies could very well become your supporters. Allow a person to dislike you for what you've done and not because of your connection to another.

6. **Never allow people to disrespect or speak negatively concerning them.**

Never participate in any negative discussion or tolerate disrespect toward your predecessor. Even if you agree or may have the same sentiments, you will win if you digress from or remove yourself from the conversation. You don't ever want to be found guilty of adding to a conversation or the communication that is not enriching or esteeming your predecessor.

7. **Compensate or reward them if necessary and if you can.**

For many older pastors or bi-vocational pastors, the reality of retirement was never on their radar. Many pastors literally die in their pulpits as they witness the rise and fall of their congregation, but they remain because they are not financially prepared to live otherwise. I would first advise newcomers to make sure that you begin planning now for retirement and life after the pastorate. If your annual budget affords you this privilege and there is currently no compensation being awarded to your predecessor, discover creative means of supplementing their income. This can be done by affording them with an annual day, special offerings (of course within IRS regulations) and personal gifts which can be awarded to them.

CHAPTER FIVE

The Burden To Empower Others

"A leader is great, not because of his or her power, but because of his or her ability to empower others. Success without a successor is failure."

Toler & Nelson- authors of *The Five Star Church*

Chapter Five ~ The Burden To Empower Others

The early church had two offices to govern its affairs which were the office of bishop/elder and the office of deacon. It was the belief of the early church that an official governing board serving the people of God was a necessity in order that the church might be functional. Then and even now, the eldership was the responsibility of the pastor and the lay leadership of the church was vested in the "board of deacons." In the life of the church, especially as it relates to lay leadership, the deacon has been an essential personality. Howard Foshee, in his book, *Now that You're A Deacon* writes, "As Baptist churches were established in America during the eighteenth and nineteenth centuries, deacons played a significant leadership role in the life of these churches. Being servants of the church, as the very word "deacon" implies, they served wherever there was a need."

The Role Of The Deacon

The word or title deacon is a Greek word that the New Testament writers borrowed and developed as a part of their vocabulary. The word "diakonas" depending upon the context is translated either as "deacon" or "servant" and a similar word "diakonia" which is usually translated "ministry" or "service." In the early days, the word "deacon" referred to waiting on tables, but it later broadened to include the idea of providing or caring for any need of another person in a personal way. The work and the call of the deacon in the early church were established as the result of a need in the church. Foshee further sheds light regarding the problem that developed in the early church:

"As the early church in Jerusalem grew rapidly, there arose a "murmuring" among some of the members. The misunderstanding arose between Jewish Christians who continued to follow ancient Hebrew traditions and other Jewish Christians who had accepted the language and social customs of Greece and Rome. The actual misunderstanding developed over the methods used for administering the daily food distribution to their Jewish widows. The incident, as recorded in Acts 6, was only an outward symptom of a deeper problem. The major problem was a potential break in Christian fellowship."

Deacons, now commonly identified as the diaconate, have been an active participant in the continuing vitality and strength in many religious traditions, including the United Methodist, Roman Catholic, Episcopal and Baptist churches. In the Baptist church, deacons maintain various standards of lay leadership primarily because our theology affirms the role of the laity, and our churches are organized margining democratic principles. In some Baptist churches the duties of the deacon have included handling familiar functions of the church such as the preparation of the elements for the Lord's Supper and assisting the pastor in serving the elements to the congregation; conducting devotional or prayer gatherings; caring for Baptism candidates; and providing for the pulpit responsibilities of the church in the absence of the pastor. In other churches, their responsibilities extend to performing many secular functions regarding finances and property concerns.

In the Baptist church, deacons are selected primarily in three distinct ways. They can be identified and/or proposed by means of a nominating committee, by the vote of the church or upon the recommendation of the pastor. Historically, the writer identifies concerns, which will be further considered in this section, regarding the selection, preparation and work of the deacon. Dr. Everett Goodwin, the author of *The New Hiscox Guide for Baptist Churches*, writes:

"There are two problems associated with the service of modern deacons. The first is that in some churches deacons become little more than honorary, ritual leaders, often chosen only from the most senior members of long standing and with little official or unofficial purpose. The second problem is that in many Baptist churches the diaconate has developed into the "power center" of the congregation and can exercise an unbiblical tyranny over the church and, in some cases, the pastor. In such cases, diaconal ministry reverses the role established in Acts by making the servants in fact the supervisor."

In my dissertation, which presented a new paradigm for developing lay leaders for church growth, I endeavored to research other works that have addressed or have considered the subject matter concerning leadership. John Maxwell argues in his work, *The 21 Irrefutable Laws of Leadership*, that:

"Leadership is leadership no matter where you go or what you do. Times change. Technology marches forward. Cultures vary from place to place. But the true principles of leadership are constant--place to place."

While I agree with Maxwell's belief regarding the continuity of leadership, my concerns are with the persons responsible for preparing these future leaders. Dr. Goodwin acknowledges and the writer agrees "...churches and church leaders are challenged to create leadership channels that enable the congregation to accomplish its goals without exhausting the spirit of the church."

Historically, some leaders in the life of the local church have failed or have not risen to the occasion of performing their expected and respective roles as the leading men and women of the local church. This is due to inadequate training or simply no programs for leadership provided by pastors. On the contrary, I purport that the church has always been a nurturing and/or developing station, notably the black church, where intentional and unintentional lessons have been learned. Henry Young writes in his book *Major Black Religious Leaders*:

"...the Black Church has always been a source of identity for Blacks. They discovered that the opportunity found in the Black Church to be recognized as somebody of value and dignity, and to possess a position of importance, has stimulated pride and preserved self-respect in Blacks who otherwise would have been entirely beaten and completely submerged by their existence. Both socially and psychologically, every person has a need for recognition and importance. Historically, the Black Church has supplied this need."

Again, I agree that the black church has always been a great resource in the developing of its people, but the writer's argument has been the lack of intentional and constructive programs designed to assist those who are the leaders within the church. The intent of this chapter is to identify historically why leaders, particularly in the life of the local church, failed or have not risen to the occasion of performing their expected and respective roles as the leading men and women of the local church.

While attempting to search previous models of creating productive leadership within a local church, I was privileged to consider the life and ministry of the Reverend Fred Shuttlesworth, a civil rights leader and pastor in Birmingham, Alabama. Andrew Manis, the author of *A Fire You Can't Put Out*, reflected upon Shuttlesworth's recommendations for the Revelation Baptist Church:

"He expected to build a church with ample educational and recreational facilities, a church bus, active denominational involvement, a Baptist Training Union, a youth program, and financial pledges and building funds. More characteristic of his commanding pastoral demeanor, yet not unusual for a Black Baptist Pastor, Shuttlesworth proposed certain policies designed to keep his prospective members in line. He insisted on an annual call of trustees and deacons with no church officers to serve without the approval of the pastor and the larger congregation. All groups and persons working in the church were to be subject to the direction of the pastor."

I agree with many of Shuttlesworth's ideological propositions. In addition, I also acknowledge that Shuttlesworth is not a methodologist, a person who assumes responsibility for a systematic body of procedures or techniques as it relates to the ethos of church leadership. It was therefore difficult for me to discover what process or program he used in developing his church leaders particularly because there was no publication identified in Manis' documentation reflecting upon this distinguished preacher and civil rights trailblazer's preparation of church leaders.

I can recall an experience in one of the churches that has served as a nuance for my ministry and supports why leaders have not risen to the occasion of fulfilling their perspective targets. There was a distinguished, well-groomed and obviously wealthy gentleman who committed to that particular local ministry. The pastor and members were supportive and welcoming to the new member. Shortly after he received the "right hand of fellowship," the pastor and leaders anxiously welcomed this new member to serve as a member of the Diaconate. What a mistake! He had been a Christian for less than ninety days, yet he was offered the opportunity of functioning as a member of the official governing body of that local church. Shortly after his immediate catechism, that same gentleman's unseemly mannerism of familiar secularism was clearly evident. William Willimon supports my precaution of unprepared leadership in his book, *Calling and Character*. Willimon writes, "Lacking a sense of the peculiar shape of ministerial character, bereft of the well-formed church, we become the victims of whatever cultural images of success happen to be in ascendancy at the moment."

Another concern that I have is the perceived objective of some pastors in the training of leaders to become managers rather than leaders. John Maxwell states in his book, *Developing The Leader Within You* that:

"Management is the process of assuring that the program and objectives of the organization are implemented. Leadership, on the other hand, has to do with casting vision and motivating people."

Historically, some leaders of the church have been trained to supervise programs and to maintain the traditional routines of the church (i.e., ushers, grounds). This is simply teaching people to be managers. Where there is the element of management in existence rather than leadership, we place persons in controlling rather than equipping roles. Barna writes, "Leading is different from managing, teaching, counseling and helping. I have seen many ministries undermined by people who serve in positions of leadership, but are incapable of leading."

It is the belief of the writer that lay leadership should function as persons equipping the ministry and not as controllers. Position provides power, but the writer recognizes that power is a dangerous weapon in the hands of a person who takes advantage of his/her position. The challenge is this: How do we prepare leaders to be equippers and not controllers? The response is that the leader must employ a process. Leighton Ford writes in his book *Transforming Leadership*: "At the risk of being thought overly simplistic, one can say, therefore, that a consideration of leadership must pay attention to the position which the leader holds, the person that the leader is, and the process which the leader employs."

The Need

I have been challenged with the following questions. How do leaders come into being? Often, leadership emerges out of an unfulfilled need. Historical African-American leaders such as Adam Clayton Powell, Martin Luther King and Benjamin Mays emerged into leadership primarily based upon the need. Powell, as written by Young, "was driven toward social justice, political awareness, and sensitivity for the poor, disadvantaged, and dispossessed by parental influences and the social conditions of his day." King was persuaded as a result of Mays and his other colleagues involved in the Montgomery Boycott. This was documented in his autobiography, *Born to Rebel*, "my entire life has been centered around protest against the social evils that seek to keep Black Americans oppressed."

Again, historically, leadership was emanated based upon need. Peter Paris writes in his book, *Black Religious Leaders*, regarding Dr. King:

"Much of King's activity was aimed at the more proximate goal of effecting legislative change, chiefly at the federal level, in order to establish and protect the civil rights of Black people. Many of his critics considered his emphasis on legislative change to be far too great. King, however, was not persuaded, in spite of his knowledge of the limitation of law and law enforcement. He was never deluded into thinking that laws can change the hearts of people or that the existence of just laws is in itself sufficient for the emergence of the community of kindred human beings. However, he did believe that just laws and their enforcement could alter the behavior of citizens. King actually thought in terms of two goals for society, one being justice and the other kinship."

In regards to church leadership, we must consider the following: Does the need, or rather has the need, justified the concerns of the local church or has it ushered the local church into a position of simply operating within the rhythm of the status quo? Maybe this remains a bias of the writer, but during the writer's nurturing and involvement in the ministry opportunities of three Baptist Churches, there wasn't much evidence of the leadership operating in the capacity of leading the church by method of participation, but primarily through management. Based upon my observation of the role of the Diaconate, I am concerned that those pastors were committed to establishing exemplary ministries, but the writer can't recall an established regimen utilized in their preparation of such leadership.

We have recognized the need for the preparation of church leaders, but how is the need met? Toler and Nelson in their awesome book, *The Five Star Church*, share with us several principles that contribute to the success of a church. The following two principles aid the writer in addressing the need of properly developing lay leaders for church growth:

Principle Two: "Let's practice what we preach and put thorns in our laurels."

In other words, the authors recognize the danger of becoming, as the older saints have said, "at ease in Zion"; the perplexing position is that many of our lay leaders are in a state of complacency as though they have arrived. Many have considered leadership as a vehicle by which one will obtain stature and serenity rather than the opportunity to perform faithfully while producing the fruit necessary to maintain and accomplish the vision and mission statement of the ministry. From my own experience, this resolve for power has become burdensome as it relates to healthy church growth in that both pew and pulpit can work effectively in ministry.

Principle Seven: "The leader's job is to buy into the concept for quality concern, cast the vision and never delegate the core value."

The authors assist the writer in recognizing the role that leaders have in operating as servants to everyone else to help them find a place of effectiveness. If a church is seeking excellence, it must have trained leadership available to help others find their places of effectiveness. The authors share their convictions regarding a servant leadership model:

"Leadership isn't everything, as some leadership gurus

would have you believe. Nevertheless, leading is the single most important element for any significant organizational change. If the leaders in a church do not have the vision for quality improvement and make it a part of their outgoing agenda, it's not going to happen. Something as thorough and permeating as a continual quality improvement mindset cannot be delegated."

Serving with church leaders has its challenges. Personalities, power-struggles, envy and competition are just a few of the characteristics observable in most ministries, specifically deacon ministries. However, what should be the principle role and mindset of a person serving in the office of a deacon is this – How can I assist my Pastor in bearing the load of ministry?

> *The Deacons should be the Pastor's friends. They should be encouragers, prayer partners, sounding boards, wise counselors, the "amen" corner, care-givers and car washers if necessary.*

I've been noted as being the first ordained junior deacon to be licensed in the city of Baltimore. What an honor! At the age of 14, my pastor and church leaders witnessed my passion for ministry particularly in the area of service to both my pastor and congregation. As a deacon, I was probably more committed to a devotional life in my early teen years than I was in my early adult years. I undeniably believed that my primary responsibility was to make my pastor's duties less cumbersome by any means necessary. I have a servant's heart. This should be the heart of a person called to serve and lead God's people.

Every pastor needs to be embraced, motivated and supported by men and women who understand the burdens and weights that are inherent in the life of the pastor. This relationship shouldn't become a battle zone similar to what our President is being confronted with working with Democrats and Republicans. The Deacons should be the pastor's friends. They should be encouragers, prayer partners, sounding boards, wise counselors, the "amen" corner, caregivers and car washers if necessary. No task should become too large or too small for the deacon to handle in lessening the load of their pastor.

How can the deacons lessen the load?

- No prayer should end without praying for the pastor & his or her family.

- At least once a week, call the pastor, send an email, write a letter, etc.

- At least once a month, pray with the pastor face to face.

- At the conclusion of every sermon or other sacerdotal act performed by the pastor, affirm, appreciate and admonish him/her (even if it wasn't their best presentation).

- If the congregation is asked to present gifts to either the church or pastor, you make every effort to lead the troops. Deacons should never be left behind (unless they've been asked or assigned to do so).

- Deacons should lead at home first!

- If the pastor is away, check on his/her home, family, pets, etc.

- Deacons should always be an asset and not a liability.

- If the pastor is always counseling, correcting or saving you,

you are not ready to serve as a deacon…take a seat amongst the congregation.

- Deacons should make sure that the pastor is compensated fairly for his educational acumen, experience, training and services provided.

- Without question, the deacon should never speak an ill word against the pastor, his family or church.

- Deacons should be the first to arrive and the last to leave a church service.

- Deacons should act, speak and dress as if they are the leading men and women of the congregation at all times. (Even when dressing down is permitted, the standards of leadership must not diminish.)

- Other than the pastor's family, there should be no other consistent cheering aggregation louder than the support and encouragement that is exemplified by the deacons.

- Lastly, but certainly not least, a deacon should have a real relationship with God that is demonstrated in his life during times of worship and more importantly, when church is over.

The Message (MSG) 1 Timothy 3

¹⁻⁷If anyone wants to provide leadership in the church, good! But there are preconditions: A leader must be well-thought-of, committed to his wife, cool and collected, accessible, and hospitable. He must know what he's talking about, not be over fond of wine, not pushy but gentle, not thin-skinned, not money-hungry. He must handle his own affairs well, attentive to his own children and having their respect. For if someone is unable to handle his own affairs, how can he take care of God's church? He must not be a new believer, lest the position go to his head and the Devil trip him up. Outsiders must think well of him, or else the Devil will figure out a way to lure him into his trap.

⁸⁻¹³The same goes for those who want to be servants in the church: serious, not deceitful, not too free with the bottle, not in it for what they can get out of it. They must be reverent before the mystery of the faith, not using their position to try to run things. Let them prove themselves first. If they show they can do it, take them on. No exceptions are to be made for women—same qualifications: serious, dependable, not sharp-tongued, not over fond of wine. Servants in the church are to be committed to their spouses, attentive to their own children, and diligent in looking after their own affairs. Those who do this servant work will come to be highly respected, a real credit to this Jesus-faith.

Chapter Six

The Burden To Find The Right Help

"Your job is to get the right people on your bus, get the wrong people off your bus, get the right people in the right seats on your bus, then driving your bus ..."

John Maxwell
Leadership Guru

Chapter Six – The Burden To Find The Right Help

In almost every facet of leadership, both ecclesiastical and secular, there is basic training or preliminary teachings that precede the perspective role or position that one is preparing to attain. In consideration of this argument, I was compelled to understand how Navy SEALs are prepared and promoted for warfare. Jeff Cannon and Lt. Commander Jon Cannon write in their book, *Leadership Lessons of the Navy Seals*:

"SEALs (Sea-Air-Land) train continuously and hard. The initial SEAL training at Basic Underwater Demolition School (BUDS) is 6 months long and routinely stresses its students to such a degree that there is an 80 percent dropout rate. Following BUDS, students attend courses in parachuting, mini-submarine operations, sniping, communications, demolitions, field medicine, languages, and a wide range of other areas. By the time they enter a SEAL team and are selected for a SEAL platoon, they will have received their "masters" in unconventional commando warfare."

One could consider the comparison of the Navy SEALs to the church an apathetical approach as it relates to the development of lay leadership in that the SEALs are being prepared for warfare. I acknowledge that this metaphorical "warfare" model may not be considered appropriate, quite naturally because in some churches, the idea of a "clergy killer" has been given to lay leadership. However, understanding the approach of the SEALs in developing and training persons is exemplary as it relates to the necessity of an organization's commitment to create strong and effective leaders who are able to excel and deliver extraordinary results.

Jimmy Carter, former president and graduate of the Naval Academy, in his book, *Living Faith*, shares the "code of conduct" required for a mid-shipman. President Carter wrote:

"As a young shipman, I was instructed meticulously in a demanding code of conduct. According to my aging copy of the Blue Jacket Manual, in the performance of duties, we are expected to exhibit obedience, knowledge, fighting spirit, reliability, loyalty, intuition, self-control, energy, courage, justice, faith in our self, honor and cheerfulness. But the overarching criterion was truth-absolute truth, which was described as the final test of a man. Any form of lying or dishonesty was justification for immediate dismissal from the Naval Academy. During every one of my eleven years in the US Navy, I knew that my superior officers were judging my compliance with these standards."

> The burden some pastors have placed upon themselves is that they produce qualified men and women to operate as the steering committee of the ministry without first equipping them to become disciples of the church.

A failure that has infected the leadership potential of the local church has not been just an unclear or unrecognized need, but the ability to properly empower future leaders to become disciples of the ministry. Tony Evans, the author of *The Kingdom Agenda*, defines discipleship as "the process by which we bring all of life under the Lordship of Jesus Christ."

Discipleship was a common term in the Greek world several centuries before Christ. It was a process by which the Greek philosopher Plato taught Aristotle, who then built academies to train thinkers in Greek philosophy. These disciples would then enlighten Greek culture and later the Roman culture, teaching what they had learned in order to pattern the world concerning their taught beliefs. The burden some pastors have placed upon themselves is that they produce qualified men and women to operate as the steering committee of the ministry without first equipping them to become disciples of the church. It is the writer's belief that discipleship be a prerequisite for church leadership. The writer also acknowledges that discipleship is a process. Walter Henrichsen in his book *Disciples Are Made Not Born*, states,

"Making disciples takes time. It cannot be done through a series of lectures and a training seminar in the church, nor can reading a book do it. It cannot be rushed. One of the dominant characteristics of our modern culture is our ability and desire to mass-produce. It is so easy to take this mass-produced mentality and apply it to disciple-making. It cannot be done. Disciples are made, but not mass-produced. Each one is molded and fashioned individually by the Spirit of God."

Some pastors have failed as a result of making church leaders before empowering them to become disciples of the Lord Jesus Christ. Professor Korthright Davis, the writer's professor of systematic theology at Howard University's School of Divinity, argues in his book, *Serving with Power*:

"The critical question for us as Christians today is a simple one: what does it mean to be a faithful follower of Jesus Christ in the post-modern world? How does one do this "Christian thing," become this "Christian person," and proclaim this "Christian Gospel" by word and example? The question is simple, but the answer is complex. The Episcopal Church's catechism teaches that "the ministry of the lay person is to represent Christ and His Church; to bear witness to Him wherever they may be; and, according to the gifts given them, carry on Christ's work of reconciliation in the world; and to take their place in the life, worship, and governance of the Church" (Book of Common Prayer, p. 855). Yet such a job description hardly gets played out in full or taken very seriously by many. It is usually fast-forwarded to the easy part about worship and church governance."

The Historical Perception And Relations

In some local churches, the relationship between the pastor and leaders has not always been one of evident cohesiveness. Although members of the same team, the sad reality is that too many pastors and church leaders have not always functioned as team members. G. Lloyd Rediger in his book, *Clergy Killers*, shares the following:

"Clergy killers are masters of disguise when they choose to be. They can present themselves as pious, active church members who are only doing this for the good of the church. Often they convince naive parishioners that they are raising legitimate issues. It is not uncommon for clergy killers to hide among their allies of opportunity; members who are their friends or congregational power brokers who are disgruntled with the church."

It is my belief, that many leaders maintain the role of policing their pastors rather than protecting and assisting them in promoting the gospel and vision of the church. Historically, some churches have separated and even resolved as a result of diminishing and often destructive relationships of pastors and leaders. I've discovered several reasons why there have been barriers preventing healthy relationships between some pastors and leaders.

Obviously, there has been the issue of fear, the struggle of power, and unclear and unmet expectations with both parties. However, the writer concludes that the basis of the negligent and non-productive relations between the pastor and leaders is primarily because many pastors have not been introduced to a clear and concise model of developing lay leaders for ministry and church growth. Sharing his expectations concerning those serving with him, former President Carter wrote, "I looked upon the Navy rules and regulations as a framework of my performance as an officer, one tried and tested for hundreds of years, as the best means to ensure effective roles for my ship and crew."

The pastor and the leaders of the local church can maintain a healthy, non-threatening atmosphere if the pastors are willing to spend the necessary time preparing and mentoring the future leaders, inevitably establishing a premise by which future leaders can understand and participate in wholesome Christian leadership. Maxwell writes in his book, *Developing the Leader Within You*:

"Loyalty to the leader reaches its highest peak when the follower has personally grown through the mentorship of the leader. (1) The leader chooses the follower; (2) The follower loves the leader; (3) The follower admires the leader; (4) The follower is loyal to the leader."

I'm convinced that historically, based upon my experience in ministry, some leaders in the church have failed or not risen to the occasion of performing their expected or established roles as the leading men and women in ministry.

Furthermore, it is my belief that if there was an established training model in place within a local church, lay leadership could be more effective in fulfilling their respective roles and responsibilities. Within the realms of that model, there must be an element of preparing persons to understand that in the church, the words, leadership and service, are synonymous. Carter G. Woodson in his book, *The Mis-Education of the Negro* writes:

"If we can finally succeed in translating the idea of leadership into that of service, we may soon find it possible to lift the Negro to a higher level. Under leadership we have come into the ghetto; by service within the ranks—I'm pretty sure this isn't the right word here. Do you mean "ranks?" we may work our way out of it. Under leadership we have been constrained to do the biddings of others; by service we may work out a program in the light of our own circumstances. Under leadership we have become poverty-stricken; by service we may teach the masses how to earn a living honestly. Under leadership we have been made to despise our own possibilities and to develop into parasites; by service we may prove sufficient unto the task of self-development and contribute our part to modern culture."

The Call

There are certain factors that necessitate one's calling. The call of God is specific and unique for the purpose God has destined for life. However, the call of God has two different sides that make a completely balanced whole as it relates to the Body of Christ. In his book, *The Making of a Leader*, Frank Damazio shares that the Body of Christ has been called to both governmental and congregational ministries. He writes:

"There is a great difference between the governmental

ministries and the congregational ministries. Governmental ministries are given divine authority to rule the Body of Christ through the offices invested in them, the offices of the apostle, prophet, evangelist, pastor or teacher. To function in one of these offices, a person must receive a call from God, and under His authority, carry out His purposes. To function in a congregational ministry, a person must understand his position of responsibility and his limitations. Each part of the Body of Christ has received a call from God, but not necessarily to function in a governmental ministry."

Many scriptures in the Old Testament depict the phenomenon of so-called leadership without the call of God. Every passage concludes with the self-same end: going forth on their own initiative, without the Lord sending them, these men failed. In the book of Jeremiah, the subject concerning the call of God is substantiated. God's warnings come at a pivotal hour in the history of the Israelites as the remnant of Judah is threatened with captivity in Babylon. It is apparent that Jeremiah spoke out concerning the false prophets, those spiritual leaders of Israel who were leading the people to believe the lie that God would not punish His people for disobedience. The people later encountered disaster because they supported what their leaders had been telling them. Continuing to follow these false leaders, the prophet Ezekiel was called to respond. Jeremiah speaks:

"I sent them not, neither commanded them, therefore they shall not prosper this people at all...I have not sent them," saith the Lord. Then said the prophet Jeremiah unto Hananiah the prophet, 'Hear now, the Lord hath not sent thee, but thou makest this people trust in a lie'...They falsely prophesy, I have not sent them, saith the Lord."

Scholars have argued for centuries concerning the idea that leaders are born and not made, vice versa. Although there may be leaders and leadership models that can support either argument, it is my belief that there are three ways by which a person can be placed into leadership. First, God can appoint them; secondly, man may appoint them; and thirdly, persons may appoint themselves.

Korah, a man identified in Numbers chapters 16 and 17, is an example of a self-appointed leader who rebelled against the divinely appointed leadership in Moses. He represents self-willed and presumptuous men who want authority that has not been given to them. The man, Korah, helps us to know that a self-appointed leader takes upon him the authority and responsibility of a spiritual office into which he has not been divinely called. J. Oswald Sanders writes: "Desiring to be great is not a sin. It is motivation that determines ambition's character. Our Lord never taught against the urge to high achievement, but He did expose and condemn unworthy motivation...true spiritual leadership will never 'campaign for promotion.'"

Saul is an example of man-appointed leadership. It is the rationale of man-appointed leaders that they have received a call from God for the office for which they seek, but the call is by the authority of human vessels who are not speaking by the authority of God. Samuel was sent to the people of Israel to give the people what they wanted – a man to lead over them. It was that direction that Samuel followed. He gave them a leader appointed only with earthly authority, a ruler who could only utilize earthly resources. Saul's job description is listed in I Samuel 8:11-17.

"He will take your sons and appoint them for himself." (I Samuel 8:11)

"He will appoint many men to work in his ground, to harvest his crops, to make his instruments of war and his chariots." (8:12)

"He will take your daughters to be perfumers, cooks and bakers." (8:13)

"He will take the best of your fields, vineyards and give them to his servants." (8:15)

The key points of information of Saul's description is the term, "he will take". The man appointed leader is destined to rob and spoil the people of the Lord to accommodate his own selfish desires. Evans writes "God created us for His glory. So whenever we try to take glory unto ourselves and live independently of God, we are living well beyond our privileges."

Aaron is another example of man-appointed leadership. Moses, that fearless Israelite leader, was challenged with chaos as a result of Aaron's promotion due to Moses' unpredictable return. Exodus 32:1 is the verse where we see this example of man-appointed leadership:

"When the people saw that Moses was so long in coming down from the mountain, they gathered around Aaron and said, *Come, make us gods who will go before us. As for this fellow Moses who brought us up out of Egypt, we don't know what has happened to him.*"

The calling and anointing of David offers clarity to our understanding of God-appointed leadership. His brothers had countenance and craftiness, but David had a heart that captivated God. "Do not look at his appearance or at his physical statue, because I have refused him. For the Lord does not see as man sees; for man looks at the outward appearance, but the Lord looks at the heart."

Adam Clayton Powell, Jr. contributes the following statement that influences our awareness of God appointed leadership:

"So, with the awareness of God one looks around beyond the beauty of the superficial and truths of the relative. One looks for beauty in all things because all things come from the Creator of beauty. A chain reaction is set up, not the chain reaction that comes from the beauty of the superficial nor the truth of the unpopular word, but a chain reaction that leads to goodness from the beauty that is within and the truth that makes one free.... We are not, therefore, to be judged by the position that we hold in church, nor by our years of membership, nor by the contributions that we make to our church life. For if God looks not on the outer man, how can we?"

How Does God Choose Those Who Shall Be Leaders Within The Body?

God-appointed leadership should remain the guide by which spiritual leadership is sanctioned. We must again understand that God chooses leaders to function in given capacities. The Bible shows us that when God chooses a person to lead His people, someone who is ready to commit to full discipleship and to take on the responsibility for others, that person is used to the limit. These leaders must still face the challenges of humanity, but in spite of their shortcomings, they remain God's choice for spiritual leadership. As it relates to the challenges of leadership, Dr. Cleophus LaRue, author of *The Heart of Black Preaching* writes:

"All peoples have had to endure something. While life experiences of Blacks certainly impact and color their interactions with God and Scripture, it is the sovereign God at work in and through these experiences that characterizes the essence of Black preaching. Black Christian faith and concomitantly Black Christian preaching, involve the positive response of the total person to the initiatives of almighty God."

J. Oswald Sanders writes, "Many people regard leaders as naturally gifted with intellect, personal forcefulness and enthusiasm. Such qualities certainly enhance leadership potential, but they do not define the spiritual leader. True leaders must be willing to suffer for the sake of objectives great enough to demand their wholehearted obedience.... Spiritual leaders are not elected, appointed or created.... God makes them alone. A person must qualify to be a spiritual leader."

The Leader As Servant

Most people would say that the leader is the person who directs, administrates, organizes, makes the difficult decisions and even is the one who prepares followers for futuristic opportunities. However, this definition lacks a very essential component of genuine leadership; a leader is one

The term servant speaks of low prestige, low respect and low honor, which makes leadership unattractive, especially for those seeking status or position.

who serves. In order to understand how God clearly defines or what the writer believes is the essence of "spiritual" leadership; we must examine how the word "leader" is used in the Scriptures. The term "leader" is only used six times in the King James Bible. In fact, the word much more frequently used is the word "servant." In the Old Testament, Moses is not referred to as "Moses, my leader," but "Moses, my servant."

The New Testament uses the Greek word for servant,

"doulos," which offers an excellent word picture of a servant's heart. Generally, the word "doulos" denotes bondage, but it most commonly applies to a servant who has submitted himself to a master by some legal obligation. The Apostle Paul very frequently used the word signifying his relationship to Jesus Christ. Jesus used the term servant as a synonym for greatness. The term servant speaks of low prestige, low respect and low honor, which makes leadership unattractive, especially for those seeking status or position. A spiritual leader must have the inner attitudes and motivations, and the outer service, of a servant. However, Jesus declares, "Whoever wants to become great among you must be your servant, and whoever wants to be first must be a slave to all."

It is obvious that this concept may be unattractive to potential leaders, but it must be clearly stated that the "servant" model is His requirement for those who want to lead in the Kingdom of God. Rank and honor are not identifiable or suggestive descriptions for spiritual leadership. God designates spiritual ministry and leadership according to His sovereign will. As important as education and proper training is, effective spiritual leadership does not come as a result of theological training or a seminary degree. The wisdom of God in calling men and women to function in different positions is past human understanding and human legislation. It is established in the Word of God. In the epistle to the Church at Corinth, Paul states this doctrine of God's calling in a clear manner:

"For you see your calling, brethren, how that not many wise men after the flesh, not many mighty, not many noble are called. But God hath chosen the foolish things of the world to confound the wise, and God hath chosen the weak things of the world to confound the things that are mighty. And the base things of the world, and the things that are despised, hath God chosen, yea, and the things, which are not, to bring to nought things that are, that no flesh should glory in His presence."

It remains my conviction, that leadership is God ordained. God's leaders are always people of great courage. God's leaders are willing to journey into unfamiliar terrain and are willing to take reasonable, and often, unreasonable risks, in order to fulfill both calling and purpose. The call of God remains essential if that leader is going to be useful for the Kingdom agenda. Barna writes, "If you have been called, you will have a sense of divine selection for the task. You will have inner conviction that, as amazing as it may seem, God wants you to lead for Him and to Him."

In this pursuit of identifying the "burden bearers," I've identified the theological pattern as identified in the Scriptures regarding the choice and development of leaders. As the ultimate handbook for the believer, there are clear and concise words in the Bible, such as appoint, separate, call and send, which provide scriptural insight into God Himself calling and preparing His leaders. George Barna, the author of *Leaders on Leadership* writes:

"The need to raise up transforming leaders is matched by the opportunity. As the psalmist said, "For no one on earth-from east or west, …can raise another person up…God alone…decides who will rise and who will fall" (Ps. 75:6,7, NLT). God in His sovereignty has always raised up leaders for His people-The Moseses and Joshuas who helped His people move from Egypt into the Promised Land, the Peters and Pauls who helped the church shift its focus from Jews in Jerusalem to peoples of the entire world."

It is my belief that church leaders should be called of God to lead the people of God. Therefore, a prerequisite of spiritual leadership must be a relationship with God. E. Glenn Hinson writes in his book *Spiritual Preparation for Christian Leadership*, "The central concern of a Christian leader should be the same as that of every Christian, namely, an intimate personal relationship with God. You want to know God, to partake of the life of God, not just to know about God."

Most of the divine encounters throughout the Bible have related directly to God's call and necessity. For the Christian leader, the call of God is the point of revelation, a position where one can recognize personal foundation for purposeful ministry. Willimon states:

"All historic rites of ordination include a general examination of candidates for ministry. It is interesting that ordination begins with so strong an ethical examination and injunction. Ministry is apparently a vocation that is against our natural, cultural inclinations. Therefore, the church enjoins us to remember that we are called, that ministry is God's idea before it is ours and we must seek God's help to be faithful to God's calling."

I was challenged to consider how emerging church leadership has acknowledged the call of God. It must be noted, that unlike secular leadership, spiritual leadership requires superior spiritual authentication, which can never be generated by one's self. There must be an encounter with the Divine. There must be a call to leadership. Tony Evans writes, "Your calling is the divine mission to which God has ordained you and that he has burned into your heart and equipped you to accomplish to bring Him glory and to advance His kingdom."

A Model To Follow

David Ramey, the author of *Empowering Leaders*, states "the challenge to create a more humane yet productive social order is the heart of leadership."

For the purpose of preparation for leadership, Bishop Oscar Brown of the First Mt. Olive Freewill Baptist Church of Baltimore, in his own preparation and discipline of lay leaders, identified his prospective leaders as Leaders in Training (LITs), a term used by the writer as well. The term, LIT, supports the writer's definition of leadership. It is my belief that leadership is a lifetime commitment to study and service and it is the ability to be a person of influence. Barna quotes the following response:

"Leadership training is like a mosaic. You teach people to learn certain skills and use them to make a pattern. Then you help people to learn that leadership is an art in itself. Beyond growing skills, it is the ability to paint the picture. But then most important is to help people to see that becoming a leader is becoming God's person over a lifetime."

A model instituted and practiced by the writer was conducted in eight phases.

1) A Selection Process: These individuals were chosen based upon their previous commitment and presence in the ministry opportunities of the church. A thorough period of prayer was the prerequisite prior to the selection.

2) A Formal Interview: During this formal interview, these potential leaders in training were asked a series of questions that further examined their qualifications for leadership in the present ministry.

3) A Pre-Test: This test was in the form of short answer questions which examined these persons' knowledge in the following areas: Discipleship, Stewardship, Theological and

Biblical knowledge, their understanding of church leadership and their knowledge of the pastor's visions, church mission and current ministry opportunities.

4) A Training Model: During this period of training with me, these individuals followed a seven chapter manual which presented lessons on the following: Discipleship, Biblical Foundation, Theological Understandings, Stewardship, The Character and Responsibilities of a Christian Leader, The Vision, Mission and Need for Leaders of the Church and a concluding chapter on Worship.

5) An Enrichment Weekend: During this enrichment weekend, these potential leaders shared private moments of training at a retreat center with me and completed various assignments which examined their teamwork skills, their knowledge of the vision and their spiritual role as leaders in the church. This is usually the highlight of the entire development process.

> *You really get to know someone when you share the same roof.*

The participants literally live in a rented property with me and my wife for a 48-hour period. You really get to know someone when you share the same roof.

6) A Final Examination: This is a written examination in which these potential leaders recapture lessons presented in the training model. Each candidate must achieve a minimum 90% proficiency.

7) A Formal Catechism: During this catechism, current church leaders of the context and other local pastors and invited church leaders are invited to share in a formal verbal examination which again displays these individuals' knowledge of the manual.

8) An Elevation Worship: During this worship service, family members, church members and friends were invited to share in the elevation of these persons from lay members to lay leaders of the ministry.

The Results

This model has proven successful in the two pastoral contexts led by the writer and, without a doubt, has impacted the ministries in observable ways. The participants were thoroughly prepared to lead the congregation to higher levels of spiritual development. Each of the participants, with enthusiasm, completed each phase and conformed to the expectations of the training model. Each participant's perspective of ministry was broadened and enlightened in the process and each has a deepened sense of many of the norms and ethos concerning the dynamics of operating a church pursuing excellence in ministry. They each have augmented ideals of what it means to serve the people of God while working together as members of the church leadership team.

> *The participants also have a sincere desire to support and follow the vision of the senior pastor and also recognizing their responsibility to compel and encourage the membership to also follow the senior pastor as he follows God.*

The participants also have a sincere desire to support and follow the vision of the senior pastor and also recognizing their responsibility to compel and encourage the membership to also follow the senior pastor as he follows God. Many of the individual strengths and gifts of the participants were manifested as a result of the process. In addition to their strengths being exemplified, many of their areas of growth, which were stated in the initial phases of the process, were also strengthened as a result of the process.

Both congregations are now further along than before in their endeavors to meet the needs of the congregation and the community. The congregation has also embraced these individuals and now has a clearer understanding of why these individuals were chosen to participate in the leaders in training process. Because of the thorough training and outstanding accomplishments of these individuals while participating in the process, several other members have now been compelled to share in the development of our ministries and have sought participation in such a process.

I've been able to deepen my interpersonal skills as I've worked earnestly in the development, strengthening and preparation of each group of new leaders in both contexts. Many of these individuals had no relations with each other prior to the process, but are now working together as a ministry and not as a board. As a result of this process, I've been afforded the opportunity of developing a group of individuals who genuinely desire to see their church move from mediocrity to being a ministry that exemplifies excellence and embraces the vision of the senior pastor without equivocation.

Chapter Seven

The Burden Of Overcoming The Chattering Crowd

*"But they kept shouting back,
"Crucify Him! Crucify Him!"*

Luke 23:21 (The Message)

Chapter Seven – The Burden Of Overcoming The Chatter In The Crowd

When The Cheering Stops

One of the greatest opportunities I frequently witness as an ordained minister of the gospel is the privilege of meeting brides and grooms at the altar. As a clergyman, I have the awesome and wonderful opportunity of witnessing them as they share vows and make life time promises together. I am afforded the opportunity of seeing their family and friends, dressed and made up, picturesque and prepared. Weddings are interesting, especially these days. I've seen all types and kinds of tattoos on women as they sashay down the center aisle of the sanctuary. During pre-matrimonial sessions, I've heard several crazy stories in my office about bachelor and bachelorette parties which almost led me to call the wedding off. Weddings are interesting, but most of them, if not all of them, have similar outcomes.

Most weddings never seem to begin according to the time printed on the invitation. For some reason, the limousine arrives later than scheduled. The make-up and hair are most often never completed on time. Most recently, I witnessed the delay of the ceremony because the groom had misplaced the wedding rings.

Secondly, weddings are hardly ever coordinated as

planned. They are never perfect. I don't care how much planning is done prior to the day of the ceremony, something will always happen that's not part of the plan. Whether it's the missed-measurements of the runner, the fear of the ring bearer or the flower girl fails to walk down the aisle as practiced. Weddings are wonderful, but my concern for too many engaged couples and newlyweds is that they spend so much time preparing for a wedding that they fail to plan for the marriage. Many people plan for the day, spend thousands of dollars for a day, but then leave the wedding and can't even enjoy each other's presence because they are stressed out and/or burdened financially because they can't afford to pay the bills which quickly follow the wedding day.

Maybe you can't relate to being married because you've never been married, but I hope that you've at least dated someone before. If you've ever dated, you know that in the beginning things are almost perfect. The sisters will lovingly observe that "he" can't do anything wrong. If he's late, you forgive him. If he's not dressed properly, you still compliment his awful, outdated and tacky outfit. Most men would agree that we do the same. In the beginning every time she called, with excitement you picked up the telephone and said, "Hello!" In the beginning, it didn't matter if she wanted Burger King or Ruth's Chris, you made it happen. But after a few days, sisters would agree, that if he was two minutes late, you had an attitude. Brothers would agree, that the same calls you once loved receiving are now causing you to say, "What does she want now!"

Maybe you've never been married or maybe it's been years since you've dated, but I'm sure you know what it feels like to have a new position or to work on a new job. The first few days are always wonderful. People are nice to you.

People are patient with you. People are courteous to you and will go far and beyond the call of duty to assist you. In the beginning, you love going to work. You arrive early and don't mind staying late. However, once the thrill and hype of your new role or assignment has subsided, you soon hate punching in and can't wait to punch out, because what most of us later learned was that there is another side of the job and our new life that we knew nothing about.

We later discovered there were some additional assignments that were not on your job description. We also discovered that some people who were nice to you in the beginning, because they thought that if they hooked up with you, that you would look out for them. They were people in your life and circle who ascribed to the Latin phrase "quid pro quo" which interpreted means *"you scratch my back and I'll scratch yours."*

All of us have had picturesque and enchanting moments that can be compared to a honeymoon. There are no arguments. There is no fussing. There is no confusion and certainly no fighting. Nevertheless, what many of us are learning more and more every day is that just like the weather changes and just as time changes, so do things, people and situations.

Maybe that's why the Christian song writer once penned these words, "Time is filled with swift transition. Naught on earth unmoved can stand. Build your hopes on things eternal. Hold on to God's unchanging hand."

A notable characteristic and attribute of God is that He is immutable. He never changes. His love never changes. His commitment never changes. His faithfulness never changes. His grace, that amazing grace, never changes. His favor, it never changes.

Matter of fact, we serve a God who seems to never cease to amaze us. He provides strength during our weakest moments. He comforts and affirms our inadequacies. He always has the right tools to work a thing, when the thing ain't working. There have been numerous nights when I thought that there was no hope and that throwing in the towel and waving the flag of surrender was all there was left to do. However, it was during those times and seasons in my life when I had to trust that His promises are both yea and amen!

I'm glad that God doesn't change.

In my profession, my entire life focuses on the behavior and psychosis of people. If you know people like I've known them, you are already acquainted with certain characteristics concerning "us." Most of us are moody, indecisive, never satisfied and often guilty of being "sometimey."

My entire career and calling is centered on discovering new and creative ways of working with people. It is mind boggling when I consider the number of pastors, preachers and church leaders who desire to lead in church, but who haven't discovered that communication and the tone and tenor of our conversation is more than just a notion. When you are serving and/or working in the church, you must learn and discover new ways of working with all kinds of people--the good, the bad, the ugly and the people just like you. I've been in church long enough to recognize that no personality in the church shocks or catches me off guard. I'm appreciative of the anointing that God has given me that enables me to work with all kinds of people. Often, God will use the people around you to validate your spiritual maturity. He uses people to test the temperature of your own growth. Your response and dealings with people is often the litmus test that determines how anointed you really are.

CYA (Cover Your Anointing)

It's your anointing that keeps you from cussing them out. It's your anointing that keeps you from going postal. It's your anointing that gives you the strength to speak even when you really don't want to. It's your anointing that gives you the strength to walk away when your feet would rather remain.

One of the many lessons learned from studying the life of Jesus is that during his life on earth, He learned and mastered His ability of displaying compassion and love toward people even when the favor wasn't returned to Him. There were numerous encounters when there was no reciprocity being shared. Judas became the greatest Biblical "sell out", but Jesus still called him "friend." Peter denied Him three times, but Jesus still loved him so much so that after the resurrection, He informed the small crowd of witnesses, "Go tell Peter!"

> *One of the reasons why Americans should consistently pray for our president and first lady and why Christians should pray for their pastor and first family is because almost every person in leadership has a crowd often times quietly, loudly and almost stubbornly screaming "Crucify Him, Crucify Him!"*

James and John couldn't keep their eyes opened during the midnight watch, but Jesus still looked out for them. The Palm Sunday crowd quickly changed their opinion of Him, but He continued His commitment and fulfillment of dying on the cross.

Annually, during the Passion season, I am reminded of how quickly people change. The same people who celebrated Jesus' arrival were the same ones who expedited His departure.

One of the reasons why Americans should consistently pray for our president and first lady and why Christians should pray for their pastor and first family is because almost every person in leadership has a crowd often times quietly, loudly and almost stubbornly screaming "Crucify Him, Crucify Him!"

Our current president has remained successful in overcoming the senseless and unwarranted attacks against his leadership endeavors and responsibilities. More importantly, in the Gospel of Luke, Jesus offers us a strategy and an approach of effectively responding to the crowd even when the cheers have concluded.

The first lesson shared by Jesus during His moments of criticism and ostracism was this:

Stick To The Script

I want to admonish everyone who has been blessed with a burden to commit to never rewriting or removing yourself from the script that has been created and designed for you. Many times the journey can cause us to wonder if we are headed toward our anticipated destination. Please don't lose your focus while on the journey. The Bible says "The race is not given to the swift…neither to the strong…"

Jesus was masterful in sticking to the script. Even in times of frustration and moments when His Divinity was consumed by His humanity, Jesus would resolve to saying "Nevertheless, not my will, but Thine be done."

God is methodical in using our scripts to stretch us and prepare us for greatness. Preparation is the first cousin of Elevation. God is creative and masterful in developing us during moments of chaos. For many people, courage is born in chaos. God occasionally allows adverse situations to serve as the conduits He uses to catapult us in the direction of greatness. He uses pain to develop peace; storms to strengthen and increase our faith; He affords us seasons of lack to teach us to appreciate seasons of plenty; He uses moments of brokenness to establish unspeakable joy; He permits seasons when we feel powerless to affirm the anointing He has given us. Simply and more commonly stated, *no test--no testimony*.

God uses the script to stretch you, but He does it because He just wants to know, can you be tested? Can you be tried? Can you go through hell and still be able to stick to the script? You've been blessed with a burden, but you must never forfeit or fail to stick to the script that God has for you. It's not always easy, but stick with it. It won't always seem fair, but stick with it. Regardless of the details and the drama concerning your script, stop deliberating and just commit to making the best of what often feels like a messed up situation.

My friend, if God didn't think that you could handle the script, He would have given the script to someone else. It's your script, work it!!!

One of my favorite poems is the poem *If* by Rudyard Kipling:

> *If you can keep your head when all about you*
> *Are losing theirs and blaming it on you,*
> *If you can trust yourself when all men doubt you,*
> *But make allowance for their doubting too;*
> *If you can wait and not be tired by waiting,*
> *Or being lied about, don't deal in lies,*
> *Or being hated, don't give way to hating,*
> *And yet don't look too good, nor talk too wise:*
> *If you can dream - and not make dreams your master;*
> *If you can think - and not make thoughts your aim;*

If you can meet with Triumph and Disaster
And treat those two impostors just the same;
If you can bear to hear the truth you've spoken
Twisted by knaves to make a trap for fools,
Or watch the things you gave your life to, broken,
And stoop and build 'em up with worn-out tools:

If you can make one heap of all your winnings
And risk it on one turn of pitch-and-toss,
And lose, and start again at your beginnings
And never breathe a word about your loss;
If you can force your heart and nerve and sinew
To serve your turn long after they are gone,
And so hold on when there is nothing in you
Except the Will which says to them: 'Hold on!'

When the cheering ceases, please commit to sticking to the script!

But the second thing that you must do is this:

Alienate Yourself From The Audience

Don't allow the response of the crowd to throw you off! Friends, the crowd is sometimes unpredictable. Sometimes they are feeling you and sometimes they are not. What I've discovered is that many times, the crowd doesn't appreciate your work on the stage. There are haters in the crowd, but there are also people (thank you, Jesus) who are in your corner and cheering you on. There are people who are praying for you. There are people who believe in you and who are supporting you.

However, what we learned during the processional of Jesus on Palm Sunday was that the audience will sometimes change their opinion of you. The Bible says that the same people who were saying "Hosanna, Hosanna" in chapter 19 of Luke, are now the same ones who later in chapter 23 on that faithful Friday were proclaiming, "Crucify Him."

One of the greatest pains experienced in ministry is the pain of being hurt by people. I wish that I could share in the affirmative concerning the inevitable brokenness and bitter reality of the hurt born out of failed relationships and the disappointments that will become for many readers an annual testament of "oops, I did it again" moments. If you've never been hurt by people, you have no idea what I am talking about. However, most people reading this book can say, "Been there, done that!"

It was the crowd and the audience that almost caused Jesus to walk off the stage. Friend, sometimes, life and people will make you feel like walking away. They will make you feel like giving up. The temptation to quit will become inevitable. There will always be forces, always, that will increase the desire to walk off the stage. There is a remnant who wants you to throw in the towel. They are trying desperately to send you into early retirement. They want to see you fail, fall and see you caught with your pants down. However, the Bible says, "If a man places his hand on the plow and walks away, he is not fit for the Kingdom of Heaven."

If the idea of quitting was your desire prior to reading this chapter, I'm glad that God kept you alive to reach this page.

My friend, you can't quit! You've come too far to quit. You've suffered too long to quit. You've been through too much to quit. What you have to know is this: you are right now too close to quit! What is about to happen to you can't be compared to what you are going through right now!

No Matter What The Audience Says Or Does, Stay On The Stage!

When I was being initiated into the greatest and first black Greek fraternity, there was another poem that I and my line brothers committed to learning. It was a poem written by an unknown author entitled, *"Don't Quit!"*

> *When things go wrong, as they sometimes will,*
> *when the road you're trudging seems all uphill,*
> *When the funds are low and the debts are high,*
> *and you want to smile, but you have to sigh,*
> *When care is pressing you down a bit, Rest, if*
> *you must, but don't you quit.*
> *Life is queer with its twists and turns, as every*
> *one of us sometimes learns,*
> *And many a failure turns about, when he might*
> *have won had he stuck it out;*
> *Don't give up though the pace seems slow--You*
> *may succeed with another blow.*
> *Often the goal is nearer than It seems to a faint*
> *and faltering man,*
> *Often the struggler has given up; when he*
> *might have captured the victor's cup,*
> *And he learned too late when the night slipped*
> *down, how close he was to the golden crown.*
> *Success is failure turned inside out-- The silver*
> *tint of the clouds of doubt,*
> *And you never can tell how close you are. It*
> *may be near when it seems so far,*
> *So stick to the fight when you're hardest hit—*
> *It's when things seem worst that*
> *you must not quit.*

My friend, rest if you must, but don't you quit! The reality concerning some of the people in the audience is that the reason why some of them don't want you on the stage is because many of them want to take your place. We used to call them backstabbers. They smile in your face and all the time, they want to take your place.

There are people who are mad at you because you are on the stage doing your thing. You are doing it big and you're doing it good! Instead of responding to the crowd, just commit to doing your!

Do it up and do it big!!!!!!!

Break the rules! Go against the grain! Create new traditions and customs! You must refuse to allow the people in the audience or the people in the crowd, to dictate what you do on the stage.

Only Take Directions From The Director

What you must remember concerning the Director is that the Director already knows the script. The reason why you received the part was only and all because the Director knew that you could work the script! Listen, not everyone can do what you do. The reason you have the script is because God knew that no one else can do this part of the script like you can!

The Director gave it to you because He knew that you could handle it! What you also need to know is that it's not always the people in the audience who hate on your skills, but sometimes it's also the people on the stage with you who are upset because they don't have your part. Don't lose too much sleep or waste too much time anticipating their validation. The reason why they don't have your part is because they don't have the skills, the anointing or the favor that you have.

So the next time somebody hates on your stage performance, just tell them that "if you want what I have, please be willing to go through what I've been through."

With this blessing, you will deal with the haters in the audience, as well as the haters on the stage. Well, how do you remain focused with so many external distractions? How do you remain committed during moments of chaos and confusion? How do you maintain your swagger, when ministry has lost its momentum?

When you strive to be just like Jesus, there will be people calling you a criminal, though you've done nothing wrong. How can you contend with the crowd who one minute is cheering you, but the next minute, they are stoning you? How can I deal with my spouse who greets me with a kiss one day and doesn't even want to hold my hand the next day? How can I work on a job where people are always in the corner talking about me? How can I serve on a ministry where the people are jealous because I have gifts that others wished they had?

My friend, if you've been blessed with this burden, the only answer or response that I can offer you is to just listen to the Director (God). Sometimes the Director will give you some strange directions. He will tell you to love them who hate you. He will tell you to pray for them who spitefully use you. That's alright! No matter what He tells you to do, just do it!

**Listen To The Director And Allow
The Director To Do His Part**

I am reminded of a story of a flight attendant who had just closed the doorway to the plane. As the plane had been cleared for take-off, she noticed a snake on the plane. She quickly phoned the pilot and informed him with much fear and tremble that there was a snake on the plane. The calm and composed pilot responded to the flight attendant by saying, "Stay calm, don't panic and listen to my voice."

> "Stay calm, don't panic and listen to my voice."

She exclaimed, "Please do something! The snake is hissing and headed in my direction!"

The pilot repeated his statement. "Stay calm, don't panic and listen to my voice."

As the plane started to ascend into the air the flight attendant again observed the movement of the snake. However, as the plane continued to ascend, the snake became increasingly more and more immobile. She later noticed and communicated her observations to the pilot. She said, "Sir, the snake for some reason is now dead."

The pilot said, "I'm sure he's dead. I told you to stay calm, don't panic and listen to my voice." The pilot then shared with the flight attendant that before he was a pilot, he studied veterinary science and what he learned in his study was that snakes can't survive at high altitudes.

To this end, for those of us who've been blessed with this burden, I commend you to keep soaring. Listen to the Director. The Director will help you bear the burden.

~He will….make your enemies…your footstool!

~He will…fight every one of your battles!

~He will make a way…out of no way!

~He will……open doors for you!

~He will….stick by you when the going gets rough!

~He will….give you joy….in sorrow!

~He will….give you hope…for tomorrow!

Listen to the Director! When you listen to the Director, burdens really become blessings because what doesn't kill you just makes you stronger!

Chapter Eight

The Burden To Balance: A Thorn, A Theory, A Testimony

"At first I didn't think of it as a gift, and begged God to remove it. Three times I did that and then He told me, My grace is enough; it's all you need. My strength comes into its own in your weakness."

2 Corinthians 12:8-9 (The Message)

Chapter 8 ~ Balancing The Burden:
A Thorn, A Theory, A Testimony

In this final chapter, I've elected to wrestle and confront the many challenges and calamities that we must daily confront and contend with as Christians. It doesn't matter how dressed up, well groomed or theologically sound we may appear while on a sanctimonious stage, the secret reality concerning every believer is that all of us are dealing with some private pain that we hope never goes public.

Each of us are most of the time surrounded by people who know what we do, but they don't know who we really are. For many Christians, our humanity thrives in secrecy trying to be presentable to those we are trying to impress. Many of us are constantly trying to build our churches and God's people while at the same time daily living through and dealing with the internal pain that we so skillfully hide while we are preaching, kissing babies and shaking hands. However, once the pomp and circumstance of our weekly dog and pony show has come to an end and all of the lights, the cameras and microphones are out of sight, reality then sets in and Superman returns to his role as Clark Kent.

For many leading men and women, the greatest moments we experience are the moments we have during our preaching opportunities. We spend unnecessary time during our sermonic preparation and delivery with an aim and effort to bastardize folk to shout because their shouting validates our voice, so we've convinced ourselves to believe. Consequently, we quickly discover that our preachment has changed no one not even the person who just finished preaching.

Undoubtedly, if we are going to secure our ministries and our churches for the future, somebody has to open the doors of the church and give the preacher the opportunity to again walk down the aisle and get saved! God cannot build a church until He builds the preacher.

In both our local and national news, there has recently been so much negative talk about our president. The polls have stated that his approval ratings are not as high as they were months ago and even now. President Obama's ratings seem to be either stagnated or continue to decrease. Each day there is more scrutiny, criticism and the development of more antagonists both Republicans and now Democrats who continue to make unethical attempts to derail his progress. Multiple attempts have been devised to distract him from his plan and to detour him from his purpose. It seems like no matter how determined he is in moving us forward as a nation, there is always some loop hole that is designed to discredit his character, his commitment and his cause. I may be among the faithful few who remain solid in our confidence, but I remain so impressed by what President Obama has been able to accomplish. I am amazed at how he is able to retain his health, remain focused on his plan, and committed to his family and constituents. It is obvious that no matter how insurmountable this journey becomes for him, the good news is that he has not lost his swagger. He is still cool as ice and twice as nice. I remain confident that he is God's man for this season.

There were those who became as bitter and bothered as I was in the first quarter of 2011 as we watched CNN in amazement to discover that the headlines in the news weren't centered on the many families in the south who had recently been stung by the rapid and unexpected tornadoes that destroyed many of their homes and businesses. The segment that we were watching on the CNN channel didn't offer any new solutions to the rising gas prices that had even preachers and church mothers cussing at the pump. Instead, this segment centered on the birth certificate of our smooth, smart and swagger-dacious President, Barack Obama.

To escalate the insult, billionaire Donald Trump was on the camera offering an interview and entertaining viewers internationally as he took the credit for being the person responsible for prompting the White House to prove that our president was really a U.S. citizen.

As an employer, I understand the significance of conducting a thorough background check, but how in the world did we find ourselves almost at the end of the President's first term in office only to have Donald Duck on television advertising his claim that we finally have proof that the President of the United States is a United States citizen.

I don't want to be accused of making that situation a racial matter, and I've not lived long enough to know all of the presidents, but I don't ever recall President Carter, President Reagan or President Clinton (now I'm glad that they didn't check President Clinton's birth certificate, because they would have discovered that somewhere in his DNA is a black man) for their birth certificates. Also, I don't ever recall either of the Presidents Bush to have to prove their citizenship.

Matter of fact, Arnold Schwarzenegger was elected to be the governor of a state that he couldn't even pronounce, and still he was elected and no one has asked him to provide evidence of his citizenship. I was appalled and absolutely disturbed that our president had his life challenged and his day interrupted over some nonsense, which he again responded to with so much class and dignity.

Credibly, what I appreciated more about our president was that he resisted and suppressed the urge to respond as many others would have concerning such buffoonery, but instead he continued to lead with class and conviction while avoiding the opportunity of having to stoop to the ignorance of another person's existence. When you know who you are, you don't have to compete with another person or lose sleep trying to keep up with another. Just be who you are. My personal mantra is "I'm only in competition with myself!"

Dr. Benjamin Mays, the former Dean of my alma mater, Howard University School of Religion (now Divinity School), and the former president of Morehouse College once said, "Whatever you do, strive to do it so well that no man living and no man dead and no man yet to be born can do it any better."

As ministers of the gospel, we are not competitors. We are not on opposing teams. We are not a group of nomads without a cause or a group of angry birds battling together, but we are in this faith thing together. Just maybe…just maybe, if we as preachers would stop competing against each other, maybe our churches would follow suit and commit to do the same.

> "Whatever you do, strive to do it so well that no man living and no man dead and no man yet to be born can do it any better."

Could the competitive influence in the pulpit be the

reason why our choirs are competing; the 8 o'clock choir trying to out sing the 11 o'clock choir…the first Sunday ushers… competing with the third Sunday ushers…the deacons…and the trustees…one acting as if they are the democrats…and the other responding as republicans.

At the end of the day we have to agree that we are all in this together! We may all be from different cities and actively involved in various associations, but if you've been tagged as a minister, you've been challenged. Dr. Samuel Dewitt Proctor would say, "We all share the burden of interpreting life's annoying vicissitudes and relating them to the larger purposes of God in creation."

Simply stated, all of us have a job that we too often just don't like!

Many of us don't just attend ministers' conferences and conventions as a result of our personal conviction to sustain and maintain the survival status of the institution. But we attend these often laborious encounters because we just need to get away from "*them*!!!"

Yes, them!!!

Let me share this divine truth. Every pastor and leader must have the ammunition and often premonition to deal with "them."

Them are the members who are never satisfied. **Them** are the members who have their mouth on everything, but won't put their hands on anything. **Them** are the ones who've been plagued with analysis paralysis. **Them** are the people who unapologetically hate you and dislike you, but **them** never leave. **Them** show up every Sunday. **Them** are the ones who will arrive early for a church meeting, but you can't pay them enough to show up for Bible Study. **Them**

are the ones who will run and shout when they hear the guest preacher who you've invited, but will sit like a bump on a log when you preach.

However, our challenge as conduits of change is how you deal with "them" and your thorn…at the same time!!!!

You see, my brothers and my sisters, most of the folk in our churches really don't understand that we've got a thorn. They really cannot fathom or understand the emotional and psychological pain that we as clergy persons deal with without ceasing.

During one of my recent sermonic meditations, I was convicted, challenged and changed by Paul's acknowledgement of a thorn which became extremely personal and problematic. In that passage in 2 Corinthians, chapter 12, Paul exposes that even pretty feet preachers of the gospel, as well as church leaders and congregants alike, must deal with a thorn!

Almost everyone is familiar with Paul. I don't believe that there is another personality in the Bible who has a portfolio, the background or the criminal record of the Apostle Paul a.k.a. the "Thriller from Manila." In Acts 8, he was highlighted for being the crazy man who was wreaking havoc in the church by arresting both men and women.

Paul had an incredulous disdain and dislike for Christians. As a matter of fact, he was on a mission to seize and destroy anyone and anybody who professed that they were followers of Jesus Christ. Nevertheless, Paul's Damascus encounter and immediate turnaround is one of the leading Biblical illustrations of how God can take the worst of us and bring out the best in us! Still, what is so paradoxical and problematic concerning Paul's transformation is another realization that every promotion has its share of pain.

Blessings are often complimented with burdens. If

many of us would have known earlier about the unexpected pressure and unbelievable pain that we are now dealing with where we are, many of us would have stayed where we were. You see, when you've been called to the light, you must be willing to stand the heat because the greater the light, the greater the heat.

Paul shares or gives light concerning three things: a Thorn, a Theory and a Testimony.

First of all, Paul shares about **The Thorn**.

In verse 7 of II Corinthians, he said, "...to keep me from being conceited, I was given this thorn, a messenger of satan to work on my nerves."

Everyone I know has at least one thing right now that's getting on their nerves and adversely affecting their life. Each of us has something. If you don't have something, there is certainly somebody. It's easy to talk about our public thorns, but most of us have some private thorns. Some of our thorns are so private, that if God didn't know about them, we wouldn't even want to tell Him about them.

As a gift for life, each of us, have been dealt a hand of cards. In each of our hands there is one card that if we could make it disappear, it would have been gone a long time ago. All of us have something! All of us have a thorn!!!!

When you wake up in the morning, your thorn says, "Good morning." When you brush your teeth, your thorn is asking you, "What are we eating for breakfast?" When you go to work, your thorn wants to know, "Where are we going for lunch?" When you go on vacation, your thorn packs a suitcase as well.

For most of us, the time that we are able to remain "thorn-free" is when we are in the sanctum of the sanctuary. On the contrary, it's our pain that often ignites a new strength within us to perform. I've personally been able to perform at heightened levels as a result of the pain and pressure that prompted me to produce.

There are numerous preachers, psalmists and other church leaders who've preached their best sermons, sang their best and led others into greater victory as a result of their pain.

> We've all prayed and have asked God to take it away, but it's still there.

Pain is sometimes the ammunition that God uses to present us faultless before the throne of God. Often, just like Paul, we've prayed and prayed that God would give us immunity from our thorn. We've all prayed and have asked God to take it away, but it's still there.

I, like you, have prayed both standing up and sitting down and it's still there. I, like you, have prayed on my knees and on my face, but it's still there. You've read the entire Bible, spoken in tongues, attended every set free and "be loose" conference created, but it's still there.

You are not alone. All of us have a thorn. It's an appetite that we just can't disregard. It's a desire that we just can't deny. It's a habit that we just can't break. It's a memory that we just can't erase. It's a thought that we just can't forget.

For many believers, particularly preachers, the thorn that we are living with is the reality that we are just lonely. It's interesting that many preachers are always in the presence of people, but at the end of the day, we are…..lonely. Everybody wants to talk to us, but who do we talk to? Everybody wants us to pray for them, but who is really praying for us? Everybody wants us to always preach our best sermons. They want us to always showcase "A-Game" ability, but when are we afforded the opportunity to just be regular?

The burden becomes more of a challenge when acknowledging this dilemma. What do you do when you've got to deal with your thorn and your spouse? What do you do when your spouse is your thorn? What do you do when you've got to deal with a thorn and the children? What do you do when you've got to deal with a thorn and your commitments? How do you manage a thorn and aging parents, bill collectors, medical issues, friends, family and even the people in your church?

Paul says I prayed three times…God please take it away, but it's still there!

Nonetheless, Paul also has a **Theory,** which I support.

Paul acknowledges the intrinsic reality that just maybe the rationale that authorizes the existence of this thorn is the theory "to keep me from being conceited." It's there to keep us from being puffed up. It's there to keep us from thinking that we're better than the next person and to keep us from walking around as peacocks.

Some of the most arrogant people that I know are preachers. 'We *is* some arrogant individuals.' Many older preachers boldly speak of how arrogant many younger pastors and preachers are, but who do you think taught us and where did we get it from?

Beware, God has no problem humbling you. He has a strange, but unique method of conveying to us that 'we ain't all that!' God permits and allows thorns to remind us that we have not yet arrived. Could it be that God allows the thorn to send a daily reminder that we are really only human? That thorn is there to give us balance. If God only allowed successes, there would be no need for us to depend on Him.

God allows successes and failures, ups and downs, highs and lows, burdens and blessings, victories and defeats, life and death, friends and enemies, joy and sorrow, heaven and hell. However, He is such a methodical God in that everything that He does, He does it so well and with so much purpose.

Paul introduced us to his thorn, he gave us a theory, but he also shares a **Testimony**. Andre Crouch would say, "I thank God for the mountains, and I thank Him for the valleys. I thank Him for the storms He brought me through. For if I'd never had a problem, I wouldn't know God could solve them. I'd never know what faith in God could do."

Right now, however, when we reflect upon the nature and the service that has been rendered as a result of the thorn, our testimony is this, "Through it all, I've learned to trust in Jesus. I've learned to trust in God and I've learned to depend upon His Word!"

We've been blessed with this burden. We all have a thorn. We understand the theory, but thank God for the testimony. That testimony is this, God's grace is sufficient! That's great news.

When I look back over my life, there were times, when my thorn almost killed me. There were times when my thorn almost led me to committing suicide. There were times when my thorn almost made me give up on my family, the church and even give up on God and give up on His Word. There were times when my thorn almost destroyed me.

However, today I have a testimony. Amazing grace, how sweet the sound, that saved a wretch like me. I once was lost, but now I'm found. I was blind, but now I see.

The very thorn that was meant to destroy you is the very same thorn that has made us who we are. I have committed to not looking at it as a thorn. I consider it to be a gift. It's a gift because the same thorn that is suggestively weakening me is the very same source of my strength.

It's a gift!

Paul said it best – "For I reckon that the sufferings of this present time are not worthy to be compared with the glory which shall be revealed in us!" (Romans 8:18)

So my testimony at the end of my story is this, "Even after all that this thorn has taken me through, I'm still here! I'm still standing! I'm still trusting! I'm still holding on! I still believe! I'm still serving! I'm still preaching! I still have joy! This is not a burden, this is a blessing!

"It is a faithful saying: For if we be dead with Him, we shall also live with Him. If we suffer, we shall also reign with Him"

2 Timothy 2:11-12

About the Author

Reverend Dr. Anthony Michael Chandler is a native of Baltimore, Maryland. He is the son of Thomas Chandler and Queen Jones. He was educated in the Baltimore City Public School System, having graduated from the Baltimore Polytechnic Institute. He earned the Bachelor of Arts Degree from Virginia Union University in Richmond, Virginia in May of 1995. In the year 2000, he earned the Master of Divinity Degree from Howard University, Washington, D.C. and in 2003, the Doctor of Ministry Degree, focusing on Preaching and Leadership in the Black Church from the United Theological Seminary in Dayton, Ohio. He is currently enrolled in the Fast Track Executive MBA Program at Virginia Commonwealth University.

In March 2000, while a graduate intern at the New Psalmist Baptist Church, Reverend Chandler was elected as the second pastor of the New Bethlehem Baptist Church in Baltimore, Maryland. In less than seven years, the church grew from less than 50 members to more than 600 members, necessitating the need for an additional morning service and increased capital gain.

In December 2007, the Cedar Street Baptist Church of God located in Richmond, Virginia, after 52 years of being led by their former pastor, accepted God's will to have Dr. Chandler serve and lead them as their new shepherd. His charismatic, innovative and stellar leadership abilities have led this congregation of 2000+ members to pursue a deeper relationship with God while renewing relationships, replacing religiosity with spirituality and leading them in reclaiming their God ordained destiny.

In addition, The African American Pulpit published in their fall 2009 edition his sermon entitled, "There's a new kid on the block!"

Dr. Chandler's greatest joy is being married to his high school sweetheart, Taleshia Lenshell Chandler. "Lady C", as she is affectionately called, is currently completing her PhD fulfillments in Educational Psychology. Their joy has been made complete sharing as the proud parents of Anthony Michael II, Alysha Michelle and Andrew Maxwell. Stay tuned, there is so much more in store!

Need additional copies?

To order more copies of
Blessed with a Burden,
contact CertaPublishing.com

- ❏ Order online at:
  CertaPublishing.com/BlessedwithaBurden
- ❏ Call 855-77-CERTA or
- ❏ Email Info@CertaPublishing.com

~ OR ~

Contact:
Cedar Street Baptist Church of God
2301 Cedar Street
Richmond, VA 23223
(804) 648-8919
www.csbcog.org

Certa PUBLISHING